PLAY BETTER BASKETBALL

The Essential Skills for Player Development

PLAY BETTER BASKETBALL

The Essential Skills for Player Development

Dawn Smyth
Kathy Brook

FIREFLY BOOKS

A FIREFLY BOOK

Published by Firefly Books Ltd. 2019

First printing

Library of Congress Control Number: 2019941275

Library and Archives Canada Cataloguing in Publication
Title: Play better basketball / Kathy Brook and Dawn Smyth.
Names: Brook, Kathy, 1970– author. | Smyth, Dawn, 1981–, author.
Identifiers: Canadiana 20190137266 | ISBN 9781770859746
    (hardcover) | ISBN 9781770859739 (softcover)
Subjects: LCSH: Basketball—Training. | LCSH: Basketball—
    Handbooks, manuals, etc.
Classification: LCC GV885.35 .B76 2019 | DDC 796.323—dc23

Published in the United States by
Firefly Books (U.S.) Inc.
P.O. Box 1338, Ellicott Station
Buffalo, New York 14205

Published in Canada by
Firefly Books Ltd.
50 Staples Avenue, Unit 1
Richmond Hill, Ontario L4B 0A7

Cover and interior design: Gareth Lind
Instructional Photographs: Christian Bonin

Printed in Canada

 We acknowledge the financial support
of the Government of Canada.

CONTENTS

Introduction

FROM THE DRIVEWAY TO THE COURT

There will always be more to learn about basketball. There will always be ways to improve your game. You could be a young player who just bought your first pair of shoes or a coach looking for effective skill development drills. Maybe you're trying out for the varsity squad, or you just want to score a few more buckets while playing your next pickup game. No matter who you are, the following pages explain how to build the skills and master the concepts needed to play this great game. *Play Better Basketball* is for anyone who wants to make an impact on the court.

Let this book guide you, inspire you and help you become a better player. We created *Play Better Basketball* with athletes in mind and to teach players how to set goals and achieve them. We organized the chapters around different aspects of the game, beginning with the basics of footwork and shot form and building to more advanced 1-on-1 skills and conditioning drills. In each chapter, after reading about various skills, you will learn different drills or activities to practice, which will help you develop what you've learned, either individually or with friends. Each drill and activity is focused on decision-making, which is key to translating your new skills into a basketball game. Regardless of what level of player you or the athletes you coach are you will find practical knowledge — this book has something for everyone.

The best players are detail oriented, and the details outlined in this book will separate you from other players. Pay attention to the key points in the skills and drills sections; they will help you further refine your game.

Read these chapters over and over. Come back to them later, and use them as a reference to keep track of your improving skills. These drills and activities have built-in modifications to challenge your development as your skill set grows. Don't forget that reading this book and understanding the skills is only part of the equation. You need to get out there, challenge yourself and put what you've learned to the test.

So lace up your kicks, grab a ball and this book and get your game on. It's time to play better basketball.

"When opportunity comes it is too late to prepare."
JOHN WOODEN

1

THE FUNDAMENTALS

To play better basketball, you need to understand the fundamentals of the game. This includes the lines and areas of the court, stances, footwork and rules. Read this chapter carefully and ensure you have a solid grasp of the concepts before moving on. Each of the following chapters builds off these concepts. The fundamentals are always important — the pros incorporate them into their daily training routines. You too must have the basics down before tackling more advanced concepts.

> *"You can have all the physical ability in the world, but you still have to know the fundamentals."*
>
> **MICHAEL JORDAN**

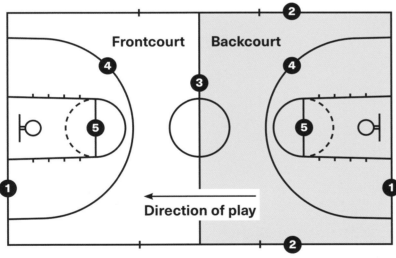

LINES ON THE BASKETBALL COURT

1 End line   **3** Centerline   **5** Free-throw line

2 Sideline   **4** 3-point line

The terminology that will be used in this book is taken from the Federation International Basketball Association (FIBA). It is the rule set used for the World Championships, the Olympics and most professional and amateur basketball organizations around the world.

THE COURT

AREAS OF THE COURT

Backcourt

Your team's backcourt consists of the basket you defend and the part of the playing court limited by the end line behind your basket and the sidelines up to the centerline.

Frontcourt

Your team's frontcourt consists of the basket you're trying to score on and the part of the playing court limited by the end line behind your opponents' basket and the sidelines up to the centerline.

3-Point Field-Goal Area

Scoring a basket from within this area results in 3 points for the offensive team.

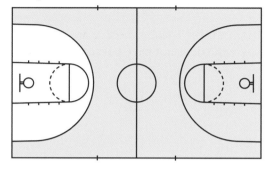

2-Point Field-Goal Area

Scoring a basket from within this area results in 2 points for the offensive team.

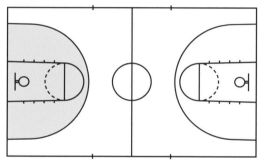

Basketball Key or Restricted Area

A player on the offensive team is allowed to occupy this area for 3 seconds at a time. When the offensive player leaves this area and returns, a new 3-second count starts.

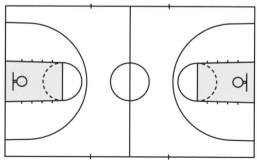

AREAS OF THE COURT AND OFFENSIVE SPOTS

1 **Elbow:** Where the free-throw line and the side of the key meet

2 **Block:** The thick rectangle on each side of the key

3 **Front of rim:** Directly underneath the front of the rim

4 **Split line:** An imaginary line splitting the court into left and right sides

5 **Wing:** An imaginary spot on the 3-point line that would meet the free-throw line (if it extended)

6 **Corner:** An imaginary spot outside the 3-point line close to the end line

7 **Top Spots:** Imaginary spots where the sides of the key would extend to the 3-point line

Low post: The area between both blocks in and around the bottom of the key.	**High post:** The area in and around the free-throw line and the top of the key.

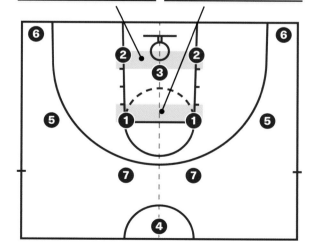

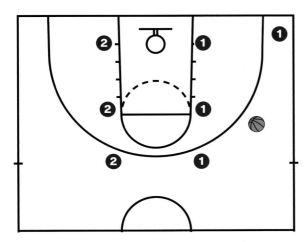

ONE SPOT AWAY OR TWO SPOTS AWAY

- **One spot away:** If a player with the ball is in the right wing spot, one spot away could be the right corner, the right top spot or the right high- or low-post spot.
- **Two spots away:** If a player with the ball is in the right wing spot, two spots away could be the left top spot or the left high- or low-post spots.

DEFENSIVE TERMS

- **On ball:** You are *on ball* when you are guarding the offensive player who has possession of the ball.
- **Off ball:** You are *off ball* when you are guarding a player who does not have possession of the ball.

Game Speed

Practice a skill at the speed you would perform it when there are shot clocks, game clocks and defensive pressure. It is easy to get complacent while practicing, but push yourself to practice at game speed. It is a tricky balance to increase your speed and keep proper form, but it is the only way to end up with great form at game speed.

BASKETBALL STANCES

ATHLETIC STANCE

Almost every single move you will make in basketball, whether it be offensive or defensive, starts in the athletic stance. This stance is the starting point for shooting, passing and playing defense. Players in this stance are in a better position on the court which improves their vision and decision-making. They are more balanced and can create more power and explosive movements on offense and defense.

The athletic stance is something that has to be learned and practiced repeatedly. Force yourself to be in this stance until it is an automatic, unconscious response to being in a game. The best players, from beginner to professional, are almost always in an athletic stance. All players should take pride in getting into and staying in an athletic stance.

 Key Points

- Feet shoulder-width apart
- Knees bent
- Seated position so that knees do not go over toes
- Hips slightly hinged, ensuring shoulders are between hips and knees
- Shoulders back
- Elbows bent and hands up, ready to act
- Head up

Top left pocket

Lower left pocket

Lower right pocket

Top right pocket

POCKETS

When you have possession of the ball in your athletic stance, you should hold it in one of your four pockets. A ball in one of your pockets is well protected, and it puts you in a position from which you can quickly pass, dribble or shoot. Your top pockets are at your left and right shoulders, and your bottom pockets are at your left and right hips.

Use one of your pockets to quickly transition to one of the phases of your shot. You will, however, need to change your hand position. Learn more about this in chapter 2.

FOOTWORK

CHINNING THE BALL

Chinning the ball is a technique used to protect your possession of the ball. You do this by placing the ball underneath your chin and both hands on the sides of the ball. Your elbows are up at shoulder height and out to the side. This creates an imaginary line from elbow to elbow, with the ball in the center. Chinning the ball is important, since it allows you to create and maintain personal space that the defender cannot enter. By placing both hands on the ball in that way, you strengthen your hold and reduce the likelihood that the ball will be stolen.

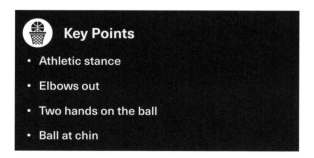

Key Points

- Athletic stance
- Elbows out
- Two hands on the ball
- Ball at chin

FOOTWORK KEY TERMS

- **Inside foot:** Your inside foot refers to the foot that is closest to the split line or basket.
- **Outside foot:** Your outside foot refers to the foot that is furthest from the split line or basket.

> The terms *inside* and *outside* are used to describe other body parts, such as shoulders, knees and hands.

PIVOT

When you receive the ball, you can only move one foot before you dribble, pass or shoot. One foot must remain anchored to a spot on the floor. The other foot can move in any direction. This action is called a *pivot*. You can only use one pivot foot, so once a pivot foot is declared, you cannot change to the other foot until you dribble.

When holding the ball, the pivot allows you to move about without traveling. It also allows you to change the angle of your body and create space and angles to pass, shoot or dribble. Always be in an athletic stance while pivoting.

Back pivot: A pivot that turns backward, in a clockwise direction.

Front pivot: A pivot that turns forward, in a counterclockwise direction.

> Sometimes you will use both the back pivot and the front pivot together, to create space from your defender or to get better court vision.

pivot foot

pivot foot

Front pivot

pivot foot

pivot foot

Back pivot

SQUARING UP

You square up when you use a front or back pivot to align your hips and shoulders "square" to the basket. This is a common term in basketball.

THE EQUIPMENT

CLOTHING

Typically, basketball players wear loose fitting, comfortable clothing that they can move in. This may include basketball shorts and a T-shirt or tank top. Some players also wear full-length or shorts-length tights under their basketball shorts or a long-sleeve compression shirt under their top. Check your league rules for uniform restrictions.

SHOES

A comfortable running or basketball shoe that allows for lateral movement and provides some ankle support is generally best. These qualities allow for the quick movements in multiple directions that are common in basketball.

BALLS

Basketball sizes vary by age, gender and stage of development.

- The men's ball is a size 7 ball (29½-inch [75 cm] circumference and 22-ounce [624 g] weight)
- The women's ball is a size 6 ball (28½-inch [72 cm] circumference and 20-ounce [567 g] weight)
- The youth ball is a size 5 ball (27½-inch [70 cm] circumference and 17-ounce [482 g] weight)

The youth ball is smaller and lighter to help ensure players maintain proper form. Using a youth ball helps young athletes complete passes with greater speed and distance and maintain proper shooting form.

RULES OF THE GAME

Adapted from the 2018 FIBA rule book.

BASICS

Basketball is played between two teams of five players each. The goal is to score in the opponents' basket and to prevent them from scoring. The team that has scored the greater number of points at the end of playing time wins.

The full FIBA game consists of quarters of 10 minutes each. If the score is tied at the end of the fourth quarter, the game continues with as many 5-minute overtimes as necessary to break the tie. The first quarter begins when the ball leaves the hands of the official on the toss for the jump ball.

During the game, the ball is played with the hands only and may be passed, thrown, tapped, rolled or dribbled in any direction. A player cannot deliberately kick or block the ball with any part of the leg or strike it with a fist.

A goal happens when a live ball enters the basket from above and remains within or passes through the basket. A goal is credited to the offensive team as follows:

- A goal released from an administered free throw counts as 1 point
- A goal released from the 2-point field-goal area counts as 2 points
- A goal released from the 3-point field-goal area counts as 3 points
- After the ball has touched the ring on a last free throw and is legally touched by any player before it enters the basket, the goal counts as 2 points

VIOLATIONS

The penalty for a violation is that the ball is awarded to the opponents for a throw-in from outside the sideline or endline nearest to the infraction.

Out of Bounds

A player is out of bounds when any part of their body is in contact with the floor, or any object, outside the boundary line.
The ball is out of bounds when it touches:

- A player or any other person who is out-of-bounds
- The floor or any object above, on or outside the boundary line
- The backboard supports or the back of the backboards

When the ball is sent out of bounds, possession is awarded to the team that did not touch the ball last.

Double Dribble

1. A player will not dribble for a second time after a dribble has ended. A dribble ends when the player touches the ball with both hands simultaneously or the ball comes to rest in one or both hands.
2. There is no limit to the number of steps a player may take while dribbling when the ball is not in contact with their hand.

If a player dribbles the ball a second time after ending a dribble, the ball will be awarded to the other team.

Traveling

A traveling violation happens when a player moves their feet or their pivot foot while holding the ball. The ball then goes to the other team.

3-Second Rule

Players cannot remain in the opponents' restricted area for more than 3 consecutive seconds while their team is in control of a live ball. The player must place both of their feet on the floor outside the restricted area to reset the 3-second count.

24 seconds

In a FIBA game, a team has 24 seconds to take a shot on the basket. This 24 seconds is called the shot clock and is often displayed on a clock on or close to the basket. Some leagues play with a longer shot clock or even no shot clock. If a team does not attempt a shot that touches the rim of the hoop within 24 seconds, the ball is awarded to the other team.

Over and Back

Once a player has crossed the centerline with the ball and both feet, they can't cross back over the centerline. This also applies to passes: a player cannot pass the ball back over the centerline. If the ball or a foot crosses back over the center-line, the ball will be awarded to the other team.

FOULS

A foul is an infraction of the rules concerning illegal personal contact with an opponent. A player can have five personal fouls called in a game. Once the fifth foul is called, that player is not allowed to finish the game. In FIBA, a team is allowed five team fouls every quarter. When a team commits a fifth foul, the other team is awarded two shots from their free-throw line.

There are several types of fouls, and the penalty awarded depends on the foul committed. Most fouls occur while players are on defense.

If the fouls occur when the offensive player is not shooting, the foul is called on the defense. The ball is then awarded back to the offense out of bounds, and the shot clock is reset. If the foul is committed on a player in the act of shooting, that player is awarded a number of free throws as follows:

- One free throw if the shot is released from the field-goal area and is successful; the goal also counts
- Two free throws if the shot is released from the 2-point field-goal area and is unsuccessful
- Three free throws if the shot is released from the 3-point field-goal area and is unsuccessful

Blocking

Blocking is illegal personal contact that impedes the progress of an opponent with or without the ball.

Contacting an Opponent's Arms or Hands

Touching an opponent with your arms or hands is not necessarily a foul. The officials decide whether the player who caused the contact has gained an advantage. If contact caused by a player in any way restricts the freedom of movement of an opponent, the contact is a foul.

Holding

Holding is illegal personal contact with an opponent that interferes with freedom of movement. Holding can occur with any part of the body. This foul can occur on offense or defense.

Charging

Fouls can also occur while you are on offense, like the charging foul. Charging is illegal personal contact, with or without the ball, by pushing or moving into an opponent's torso or pushing off a defensive player, with or without the ball, to get a better position, create more space or get free.

2

SHOOTING

Good shooting form will make you a truly great and consistent shooter. Players can sometimes succeed with poor shooting forms when they begin playing basketball. That rarely lasts. When you are in a faster game with better defenders, bad shot mechanics will limit your ability to take and make shots. You need to develop a squared and balanced stance to your shot, with proper extension and follow-through. Take the time now to develop good shooting habits if you wish to have long-term success. The best basketball players in the world still practice their shooting form every day.

"I want to practice to the point that it is almost uncomfortable how fast I shoot so that in the game things kind of slow down."
STEPHEN CURRY

SHOOTING FORM BASICS

Before you shoot, make sure you are facing the basket by using a front or back pivot to square up. You should be in your athletic stance and have the ball protected in one of your pockets.

1 Feet squared

2 Knees bent and in an athletic stance

3 Eyes up

4 Elbows in

5 Ball in pocket

This player has the ball in his lower right pocket. The ball could be tighter to his hip to better protect it.

If you have the ball in your top pocket, you will have to move it to look under it. Starting a shot from your top pocket can be helpful for a quick shot release when you are close to the rim.

In your athletic stance, raise the ball from your pocket to view the rim under the ball. This is important. If you start your shot below your eyes, it is easier for a shorter person to guard or block it. When you have a high shot release, you make your shot more difficult to guard. You want a clear view of the basket to keep focused on your target.

1. Athletic stance
2. Knees aligned with toes
3. Hips hinged
4. Elbow forward and facing the rim
5. Eye focused on the target
6. Ball elevated to the high release point

HAND AND WRIST POSITION

1 Wrist is flexed to help hold the ball

2 Fingers of shooting hand are spread

3 Ball sits on fingertips of the shooting hand

4 Thumb is not too forward, and space between the ball and the shooting hand is not exaggerated

The player's eyes are focused on the target.

Guide Hand Position

1 Hand is lightly on the side of the ball

2 Fingers are pointing straight up

3 Elbow is facing forward

The guide hand supports and protects the ball while you shoot. If your guide hand is in front, behind or on top of the ball, it will disrupt the flight path of your shot.

EXTENSION

How you extend during your shot is important for range and accuracy. From the athletic stance, uncoil your body, starting from your feet, through your knees and up to your wrists. This proper order of extension gives a shooter power and arc.

1 Ankles, knees, hips and wrists are coiled in athletic stance

2 Ankles, knees and hips start to uncoil to produce power and lift. Keep elbow and guide hand supporting the ball. Eyes stay focused on the target

3 Shoulder, elbow and wrist extend as you hit the height of your jump

Shoot the ball up from the area around your forehead to get the proper flight arc. If you shoot from the top of or behind your head, the arc will be too high. If you shoot out from your nose or below, the arc will be too flat.

27

FOLLOW-THROUGH

As the ball leaves your shooting hand, you want the last point touching the ball during extension to be your fingertips. As the ball leaves your fingertips, start to bend your wrist straight toward the target and hold the extension. This action is your follow-through. It gives the ball the backspin it needs to arc toward the basket.

1 Straight, upward extension of the arm

2 Wrist is bent and fingers are directed toward the basket

3 Guide hand is not impeding vision or affecting the flight of the ball

4 The shooting hand and the guide hand do not cross the midline of the body

The ball needs to come off your fingers last to create the proper backspin. This will give your shot a better chance of bouncing in.

Keep your fingers and wrist in line with the basket. Sometimes players will twist their wrist or fingers to one side or the other, changing the flight of the shot.

As you uncoil and extend your body, you will transfer your force to a jump. The final step is leaving the ground. You want to jump directly into the air and try to land in the same position in which you started.

Release Point

Starting your shot from a high release point will help you avoid being blocked by a defender. It takes practice to build the strength to shoot the ball from a higher release point. Start close to the basket and build up your leg strength as you increase your distance from the rim.

SHOOTING ARC

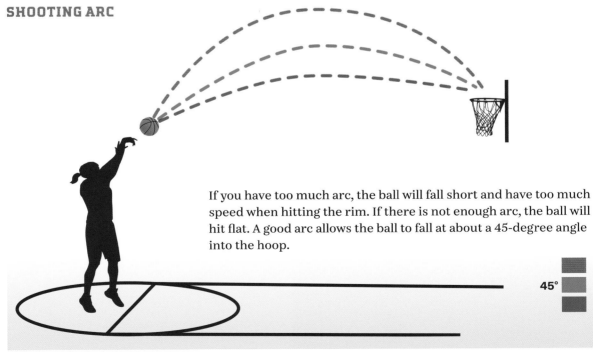

If you have too much arc, the ball will fall short and have too much speed when hitting the rim. If there is not enough arc, the ball will hit flat. A good arc allows the ball to fall at about a 45-degree angle into the hoop.

45°

SHOOTING DRILLS

WALL SHOTS

Equipment: Basketball, wall

Explanation: Stand 3 feet (0.9 m) from the wall. Shoot the ball against the wall, focusing on hitting the same spot on the wall.

Next Steps: Try shooting from 4 feet (1.2 m) away. If your arc is compromised, do not continue to move out from the wall.

Key Points

Begin in the athletic stance. Extend and shoot high on the wall. Practice uncoiling your body, and concentrate on the angle of extension as you shoot the ball from your forehead.

PARTNER LINE SHOOTING

Equipment: Basketball, line on the floor, partner

Explanation: Stand 7 feet (2.1m) from your partner with your shooting foot on the line. Shoot the ball in the air with the proper arc and shooting form. You want the ball to land on the line in front of your partner.

Next Steps: Try shooting from further apart. If the arc is compromised, do not continue to move apart.

Key Points

Begin in the athletic stance. Extend and shoot high toward your partner. If the ball does not land on the line, it may be due to the position of your guide hand or the direction of your follow-through.

This is a good opportunity to hold your follow-through. Have your partner give you feedback to let you know whether or not your follow-through is straight.

SELF-TOSS SHOOTING

Equipment: Basketball, basket

Explanation: Tossing the ball with a backspin, pass the ball in front of you about 3 feet (0.9 m). Staying low and using good footwork, catch and pivot around the ball to square up. Once square, uncoil and shoot the ball. Get the rebound and repeat.

Next Steps: Try shooting from different areas on the floor. Once your shot and release are comfortable, increase the speed of your shot to game speed. Add a defender playing light defense.

 Key Points

The self-toss needs to be in front of you. Stay low to the ground and practice your good shooting form.

One ball

Two balls

PARTNER PASS AND SHOOT

Equipment: One or two basketballs, basket, partner

Explanation: Find a spot on the floor, and square up. When you receive a pass from your partner, shoot the ball. After your shot, move to a new spot to shoot from.

Next Steps: Add another ball, increasing the speed of the shots and the amount of shots taken. Keep track of the number of shots made and the number of shots taken.

Variations: Have the rebounder and the passer switch spots after each shot. Keep track of the amount of shots taken and made in 3 minutes. Try again and see if you can beat your score.

Key Points

Work on maintaining your shooting form as you get the shot and release at game speed. Get your feet set and be "shot ready" before you catch the ball to help increase your shooting speed.

Shoot

Pass

ARMS UP, ARMS DOWN

Equipment: Basketball, basket, partner

Explanation: Your partner passes you the ball. After they pass you the ball, if they put their arms down, you shoot the ball. If your partner puts their arms up after they pass you the ball, then you pass the ball back. This drill will help you learn how to read defenses and decide whether or not you should shoot.

Next Steps: Your partner can delay putting their arms up or down until you catch the ball to increase the speed of your decision. Your partner can move closer to you, with their hands up or down, giving you less space. Keep track of your makes and misses as well as your decisions.

 Key Points

Stay low and ready to shoot. Work on your shooting form and the speed of the shot. Your feet should always be square to the basket.

3

LAYUPS

The highest percentage shot in basketball is at the rim. Often this opportunity comes in the form of a layup. Layups allow you to take a step and jump to get up closer to the rim. To beat the defense, there are many different kinds of layups that vary in direction, footwork and finishes. In some cases you will be facing the rim, while in others your back will be to the basket. To be great at scoring at the rim, you need to experiment with different steps, finishes and ways to protect the basketball while approaching the rim.

"Footwork is one of the primary prerequisites to becoming a great player."
MIKE KRZYZEWSKI

Finishes are different ways you release the ball when shooting near the rim. You can finish overhand off the backboard. You can finish underhand by flicking the ball up into the rim. Experiment with different types of finishes depending on where you are and how you are being defended. Be creative!

FACING THE BASKET

BASIC LAYUP

A basic layup is best after you beat your defender off the dribble, they are behind you and you have a clear path to the basket. This type of layup is useful in a transition offensive break, where your team has beaten the defensive team up the floor. This layup might not be as effective if there are defenders trying to make contact with you.

The motions for a basic layup are outside foot, inside foot, up and release. This layup could start with a dribble, multiple dribbles or from a stationary stance.

1 With your weight on your outside foot, pick up the ball and bring it to your lower outside pocket. Eyes are at the rim or scanning the defense and looking for teammates

2 Plant your inside foot toward the basket. Keep the ball on the outside, away from any potential defenders

3 Lift your outside leg and drive your knee up toward the basket. This generates power and upward momentum, helping you get more height on your jump. Your inside hand begins to come up to protect the ball

4 Fully extend toward the basket and release the ball with your outside hand. Don't forget your follow-through

5 A traditional finish aims for the white box on the backboard. Watch your shot

Land where you released your shot. If you land further under the basket, or even past the baseline, you did not do a good job driving your knee up. A good driving knee achieves great upward momentum. If you miss, a bad driving knee takes you behind the basket and out of the play!

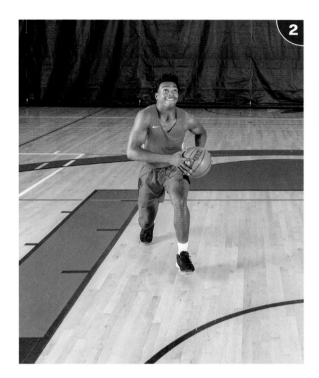

THE 1-2 TWO-FOOT LAYUP

A 1-2 two-foot layup is used when your defender is on your hip or you see the help defense coming to stop your layup. By coming to a two-foot stop before going up, you get balanced and brace for potential contact. This may also throw off a defender on your hip, leaving you open to shoot. This layup also gives you the option to gather and pass the ball to a teammate. Keep your athletic position to maintain your options.

The motions for this layup are outside foot, inside foot, together, up. The 1-2 two-foot layup can also start from a stationary position or from a dribble.

1 Take a step with your outside foot, toes facing the baseline. Gather the ball into your outside top pocket. Keep your elbows flexed and out to protect the ball. Eyes are on the target, able to scan for defenders

2 Keeping your outside foot grounded, take a step with your inside foot and establish an athletic stance. Be low and balanced to brace for contact. Stay in this position until you are ready to go up and finish

3 Lift off of two feet, jumping and extending toward the basket. The same finish as the basic layup is effective — shoot with your outside hand and protect the ball with your inside hand

4 Land close to where you took off, having converted your forward momentum to verticality by coming off of both feet. This will prevent you from running into players after you release the ball and keep you in a better rebounding position

When there is a lot of defensive traffic, get your elbows out and up when gathering the ball. Now you will own the space from one elbow right to the other. With this power position, it is difficult for a defender to knock the ball out of your hands.

REVERSE LAYUP

Having the ability to attack the basket and finish on either side of the rim makes you a difficult player to defend. A reverse layup often surprises defenders, as they are anticipating a basic layup. Once you start to attack the basket and realize that your defender is blocking your path to that side of the basket, you can start your reverse layup.

The start of a reverse layup looks the same as a basic layup and uses the same footwork. However, where you step and the angle of your body changes.

1 Attack the basket and pick up the ball when stepping with your outside foot. Take an angle that will take you under the basket

2 Take your inside step, aiming it as close to under the mesh of the basket as possible. Your hips and shoulders begin to open up to the sideline. Protect the ball in your pocket furthest from your defender

3 Now facing the sideline, explode up with your driving knee. Keep your eyes up and on the target. Use your off hand to protect the ball from defenders

4 During your jump, extend and continue to open up toward the key and foul line. The further from your body that you can extend the ball on this finish, the more distance you create between the ball and your defender

5 Finish off the backboard. Land where you took off, close to under the mesh. If you are landing far from where you took off, work on converting your forward momentum to upward momentum

Good defenders are between you and the basket. Protect the ball by keeping it in your outside pocket.

Be creative! Once you have the basics, adjust your footwork and practice layups from different angles on the floor. Change the length of your steps and how you release the ball. Play and challenge yourself to try something new.

BACK TO THE BASKET

It is a huge advantage to catch the ball at the front rim spot, on two feet and with your back to the basket. This is called the money spot because it is really difficult to guard, especially if your defender is smaller than you. This position allows you to pivot with either foot, giving you options to score to your right or your left. With practice, you will have a lot of options, and your defender will have to account for all of them.

Reminder: You only have 3 seconds in the key to make your move and release the ball.

DROP STEP

The drop step is a quick scoring opportunity that uses some of your basic layup footwork. Use this move when being defended on one side more than the other. You can often feel the defender on one of your shoulders. If not, take a peak over your shoulder to see if they are favoring one side.

1. Catch the ball at the front of the rim spot. Maintain an athletic position with both elbows up and out, protecting the ball. Feel or look for which side your defender is favoring

2. After choosing the side that your defender is not favoring, take a large step around your defender and toward the basket with your foot on that side. Chin the ball to protect it. Maintain a low stance to help your balance; there is often contact with your defender

3. Once your foot is planted, pull your other leg around and drive it up, lifting yourself close to the basket

4. Use your driving knee to gain upward momentum and align your shoulders with the baseline. Extend with your outside hand and release the ball. Keep your eyes on the target and your inside arm active to gain space to protect your release

If you turn your head and you can't see the defense, then drop step in that direction. If you take a peak and you see your defender, then drop step in the other direction.

HOOK SHOT

A hook shot allows you to shoot over your defender while creating space from your defender's arms. This works well in the middle of the key if you are as tall or taller than your defender but can also work at other angles. Consider using a hook shot if your defender is playing right on your back or if you caught the ball a little to the left or right of the rim. Don't use a hook shot if your defender is long enough to block your shot.

1. Catch the ball in an athletic stance. Chin the ball. Keep your elbows out

2. Plant your inside foot toward the front of the rim spot, with your toes facing the sideline. Begin to bring the ball up with your outside hand while keeping your inside hand up to shield defenders

3. Use your outside knee, now facing the sideline, as your driving knee. Go up straight. Fully extend over your defender. As you release, keeping your outside arm in line with the side of your body, flick your wrist to get a proper follow-through. Aim for the back rim or middle of the white square

It is key to a hook shot to use your wrist and to follow-through to get the proper arc and spin on the ball.

SQUARE UP TO A SHOT

Sometimes a front pivot to your right or left to square up and face the basket is your best option.

This gives you another set of moves after catching the ball with your back to the basket that can lead to good scoring opportunities.

You can want to make this move when you have a height advantage or can jump higher than your defender when you take your shot.

You also square up if you cannot feel your defender behind you. If you cannot feel your defender on your back, it means they are not close to you, which will give you some space when you square up to get your shot off.

1 Catch the ball in an athletic stance. Chin the ball to protect it

2 With your inside foot, take a step toward the middle of the key and away from your defender. Stay low and balanced when taking this step

3 Pivot on the planted foot to spin your outside foot around. You should be square with the basket. Keep your eyes up and the ball in your shooting pocket. Be ready to release

4 Use your legs to elevate yourself. Release the ball at full extension. Land close to where you took off

If you catch the ball on two feet, you can choose whether to pivot to the right or left side by leading with that foot on your first step. Work on pivoting to both sides and catching on both one foot and two feet to help find your pivot foot.

LAYUP DRILLS

CONTINUOUS LAYUPS

Equipment: Ball, basket

Explanation: Start by self-tossing the ball around the 3-point line. Square up on the catch and attack the rim from that angle, completing a basic layup. Get your rebound, and self-toss the ball out to the 3-point line to catch and attack again. You can't toss to the same spot twice, and your tosses have to alternate from the right and left sides of the court. Begin your attacks from different spots around the 3-point line.

Next Steps: Reduce the number of dribbles before your layup. Never do the same layup twice in a row. Add a toss to the front of the rim spot and do your back-to-the-basket finishes.

Modifications: Work from one angle on both sides of the court on one type of layup. Start the layup with no dribbles to just focus on outside, inside, up and release.

Variations: Add a guided defender who follows you on your toss. Depending on what the guided defender does, decide on the proper layup. If the defender is trailing you, do a basic layup. If the defender is tight beside you, do a 1-2 two-foot layup. If the defender has taken away your path, do a reverse layup.

 Key Points

Focus on your form and then on increasing your speed to the speed at which you would do a layup in a game.

CREATIVE CHAIR L-A-Y-U-P-S

Equipment: Ball, basket, two chairs or cones, partner

Explanation: Start by placing the two chairs in the path of a layup from the 3-point line. Call one chair "over" and the other chair "under." Your partner passes you the ball, and you do your layup, going over and under the chairs that you called out. If you make the layup without traveling, then you get an L. Make a good pass to your partner, and they can attempt to repeat the same over/under chair layup. If you miss the layup or travel, then you do not receive a letter and your partner can set up another over/under challenge by choosing new positions for the chairs. Keep switching back and forth, trying to be the player who gets all the letters in L-A-Y-U-P-S. The finish

or the type of layup does not have to be the same. The two different players could find two different solutions to going under and over the chairs and scoring. Make sure to move the angle of the layup around the 3-point line and on both sides of the half-court.

Next Steps: Move the chairs closer in a parallel line, as the closer they are to the same line the more difficult the angles are to get around. You can also have the second player or a third player be a help defender who comes across to defend you from the other side of the key.

Modifications: Keep the same over/under chairs, and try different solutions to score six times from one spot. Every time you score, you receive a letter in L-A-Y-U-P-S. Try to see if you can earn more letters the second time or in the second chair setup.

Variations: You can put defenders in place of the chairs, who can tap and reach for the ball as you go around them. This will help you practice to protect the ball as you attack the basket.

 Key Points

Be creative with your solutions to get over and under the chairs, and visualize that they are defenders in a game.

4

DRIBBLING

Dribbling is essential if you want to move with the ball from one place to another. It involves bouncing the ball with one hand. It is important that you don't dribble too much. When you choose to dribble, it must be purposeful.

> *"I dribbled by the hour with my left hand when I was young. I wasn't dribbling behind my back or setting up any trick stuff, but I was laying the groundwork for it."*
>
> **— BOB COUSY**

BODY POSITION

Body position is key to being an effective dribbler. A proper body position will give you the balance, speed and protection you need to succeed. The following are key to dribbling:

- Good athletic position, knees bent
- Head is up
- Ball does not go above waist height
- One hand is on top of the ball, and only the fingertips direct the ball back down to the ground

The opposite arm and hand protect the basketball. The ball is is dribbled close to the dribbler's body for protection from the defense.

In order to be a good dribbler you must:

- Keep your head up to see where you are and where the ball needs to go

- Be a good problem solver to understand when you should start to dribble and when it is best to stop

- Have confidence in your ability to control the ball

- Have an arsenal of dribbling moves available to use depending on the defense

- Be able to protect the basketball while dribbling

- Be able to scan while dribbling so you can see your teammates and the defense

You may use a dribble to:

- Advance the ball up the court
- Create a better passing angle
- Create a better shooting angle
- Drive to the basket
- Beat a defender

DRIBBLING MOVES

CONTROL DRIBBLE

Use a control dribble when a defender is near to you, generally in front of you. Your body and hips are turned, and the ball is close to your body. The opposite arm of the hand dribbling is up to protect the ball, your head is up and your eyes are scanning the action on the court. Bounce the ball low and hard so that the defender cannot take it. It is important to maintain a low athletic stance.

SPEED DRIBBLE

Use a speed dribble when the defender is trailing you or you have an open court and want to cover a distance as quickly as possible. A well-timed speed dribble creates separation between you and your defender. Push the ball at a 45-degree angle in front of you so you can increase your speed and advance the ball. Your head is up, and your body is also on a 45-degree angle. You may use either hand or switch between hands.

CHANGE OF DIRECTION AND CHANGE OF SPEED

Use changes of speed or direction to create advantages over the defense. Two excellent change of direction techniques with dribbling are a crossover and an in-and-out. An excellent change of speed technique is a hesitation dribble.

CROSSOVER

A crossover dribble is when the ball is moved from one hand to the other in front of the body, allowing you to step past the defense when you change direction. Keep the ball low and shift your body weight from one side to the other. This dribble is especially effective if your defender lunges at the ball.

IN-AND-OUT

Use an in-and-out dribble when your defender thinks you are going to crossover and change direction but you actually want to keep the ball in the same hand. Start to crossover by bouncing the ball on the inside of your foot, but instead of switching hands, use the same hand to bring the ball back to the original position. To do this, move the top of your hand over the ball as you release it to bounce and direct it back to the outside. As you direct the ball back to the outside, step past the defender on the same side of the ball.

HESITATION DRIBBLE

The hesitation dribble is key for a change of speed. In this dribble, you speed dribble toward the defender and as you approach, you slow your speed by putting your weight on the foot opposite the ball and hesitate your next step in the air to change your speed. Then, as the defender changes speed, you put your ball-side foot down to blast past the defense.

Be Creative!

There are many dribbling moves that are fun to practice and, if done properly, can be effective for getting past the defense. These include bouncing the ball through your legs, going behind your back, spinning around a defender or retreat dribbling. If you can't get an advantage on the first move, you can use a second move to great effect. Practice will make you more confident with the ball, but the key is practicing these moves at game speed while keeping your head up. The goal isn't to simply have many moves but to be able to react to and counter your defender. Understand what your defender is doing so you can perform the right dribble at the right time.

DRIBBLING DRILLS

ONE-KNEE DRIBBLE

Equipment: Basketball

Explanation: Kneel on the ground with one knee up at a 90-degree angle. Dribble the ball under your front leg, and then around your back. The raised knee acts as a blind spot. Take additional dribbles if you need to get control of the ball. This drill trains you to keep your head up, keep the ball low and have confidence in your ability to control the ball when it goes outside of your peripheral vision.

Next Steps: The goal is to complete one cycle with as few bounces as possible, ideally two. Increase your speed as you improve.

Modifications: You might begin by just bouncing the ball back and forth under one knee. Once you feel comfortable, go behind your back.

Variations: Switch directions and switch knees to train both hands.

 Key Points

Keep your head up and your back straight. Push the ball to the ground with your fingertips, and feel the ball.

CRAZY BALL CHAIR DRIBBLING

Equipment: Tennis ball(s), basketball, chair

Explanation: Dribbling with balls of different sizes that bounce differently builds confidence, feel and focus. Dribbling a tennis ball will help with control, while dribbling two balls at once will develop your dominant and non-dominant hands at the same time. Sitting on a chair while bouncing both balls works on balance and helps maintain the proper height of the dribble.

Next Steps: Use one basketball and one tennis ball. Try to move the balls forward and backward, inside and outside and cross the balls to opposite hands. Increase your speed.

Modifications: Players might begin by using one basketball or one tennis ball and build to using the tennis ball and basketball at once.

Variations: Swap in different balls with different bounces. Try to bounce both balls at the same rhythm or with an alternating rhythm. Try to do it standing or while moving. Attack the rim and finish with a layup while bouncing the tennis ball.

 Key Points

Keep your head up, push the ball to the ground with your fingertips and feel the ball. When you are starting, make sure the balls hit the floor at the same time.

CHANGE OF DIRECTION DRILL

Equipment: Chair(s), basketball

Explanation: Set chairs up like defenders, and practice your change of speed and crossover moves.

Next Steps: Increase your speed and the number of chairs. Perform the drill facing a wall, and after completing the move, pass the ball at the wall. Catch the pass, turn and go back through the chairs in the opposite direction. As you change your speed or direction, imagine what a defender might be doing to prompt your dribble move.

Modifications: Remove chairs and practice in the open court.

Variations: Use different obstacles or a real defender. With a real defender, read what the defense gives you so you can counter with the appropriate dribble move.

 Key Points

Keep your head up, push the ball to the ground with your fingertips and keep the ball close to your body.

SPEED DRIBBLE SPRINT

Equipment: Basketball, open court

Explanation: Starting on one baseline, speed dribble to the opposite baseline while keeping the ball ahead of you and in control.

Next Steps: Increase your speed and decrease the number of dribbles it takes you to get from one end to the other. Try dribbling with just one hand and then the other. Switch from one hand to the other while pushing the ball.

Modifications: Decrease your speed and increase the number of dribbles it takes to get to one end. Remember to maintain control.

Variations: Add a pursuing defender. If the defense catches you, switch roles. Finish with a layup.

 Key Points

Keep your head up, and push the ball ahead at a 45-degree angle.

CONTACT DRIBBLING

Equipment: Two balls, two players, a line

Explanation: Find a straight line on the floor. You and a partner stand on opposing sides of the line on the court. The basketball is in your outside hand, and you are in an athletic stance. You and your partner's inside arms are making contact with your elbows bent. You start to dribble the ball in your outside hand and move forward while keeping contact with your partner. You are trying to get both of your feet over the line, and your partner is trying to do the same. See how many times you can get over the line with both feet while in an athletic stance and maintaining your dribble. Keep your eyes up, switch hands and come back.

Next Steps: Use fakes, your inside-out dribble and changes of speed to get over the line.

Modifications: Start on the line with one ball. Your partner, without a ball, tries to lightly bump you off the line. Work toward more contact.

Variation: Start at half-court with the player closest to the sideline with the ball on offense and the player on the inside on defense. The defensive player is beside the offensive player, creating contact as the offense dribbles the ball toward the hoop. Once the offensive player gets to the 3-point line, they use their change of speed to attack the rim and finish depending on how the defense reacts.

Key Points

- Maintain a good athletic stance
- Do not push off with your arm or it will be a foul; instead, maintain a solid arm postilion
- Push the ball to the ground with your finger tips

SWITCH THE CONES

Equipment: Ball, two cones

Explanation: Dribbling the ball with one hand, pick up a cone with the other hand and put it back on the ground. Switch the ball to the other hand, and pick up the cone and then put it back down again. Try to stay in an athletic stance, and keep your head up and centered. If you need to look, scan with your peripheral vision and do not turn your head or look down.

Next Steps: Try to move the cone from one side of your body to the other side while maintaining your dribble. Start to move to different areas on the court while picking up and putting down different objects.

Modifications: Change the size of the objects being picked up. Use a bigger, higher object to make it easier and a smaller or slippery object to make it harder.

Variation: Incorporate different types of dribbles before or after you pick up the object. You may have to switch the object from hand to hand while performing the dribble moves and before putting the object back down. Race with a friend to gather the most objects and bring them back to your home base. Add that you have to score a basket before going back to pick up another object.

Key Points

- Keep head up
- Stay low to the ground
- Hinge at the hips but do not squat to pick up the cones

5

PASSING

Passing brings players together as a team. With on-time and on-target passes, teammates create the best scoring opportunities. A pass moves the ball up the court quickly in transition, shifts the defense, enhances momentum and builds team chemistry. Good passes generate small and large advantages for your offense. Simply put, passing is how your team will get good scoring opportunites.

> *"The strength of the team is each individual member. The strength of each member is the team."*
>
> **— PHIL JACKSON**

Passing Basics

To be a good passer, you must:

- Be on time and on target
- Focus on the whole court and your exact target at the same time
- Read the defense
- Anticipate where your teammate is going
- Conceal where the pass is going so the defender does not intercept the ball

When choosing which type of pass to make, determine the following:

- Where are you on the floor?
- Where is your defense? Where is your teammate's defense?
- Where should the ball be placed for your teammate to catch it?

ON-TIME PASSING

A good pass arrives on time. If a pass is too early, a moving teammate may not get to the ball. This could result in a turnover. If a pass is too late, your teammate will lose their advantage, as their defense will have time to react to the pass. To pass on time, anticipate when and where your teammate will be open and able to catch the ball and keep their advantage.

After you pass, reflect on whether it was too early, too late or on time. If your teammate had to change their hand position, body position or reach for the ball, then it is likely your pass was not on time. If your teammate was able to make a move quickly to shoot, pass or dribble, then it is likely your pass was on time. Don't hesitate to ask your teammates for feedback on your passes.

A technique to improve the timing of your pass is making connections with your teammate. Make eye contact, scan for your teammate's target hand and call your teammate's name.

 On-Time Tip

Always be in an athletic stance! If you're in your stance, you'll be ready to pass when the time is right.

ON-TARGET PASSING

Once you get your timing down, the next phase is to work on your aim. Passing the ball on target includes three components:

- Getting the ball past your own defender
- Getting the ball past your teammate's defender
- Getting the ball to where your teammate can catch it

To get the ball past your own defender, you need to recognize the windows created by the defender's body, arms and hands. To get the ball past your teammate's defender, you need to recognize where the defender is in relation to your teammate. For example, if the defender is close to your teammate's left hand, then the pass should go toward your teammate's right hand. You need to deliver the ball to your teammate's target hand. Whether your teammate has their target hand high or low, that is where you throw the pass.

An on-target pass to a moving teammate is passed away from your teammate's defender and in the direction of , and usually slightly ahead of, your teammate's target hand. If they are moving, you will need to lead them. If your pass is on time and on target, your teammate should have no trouble catching the pass while moving—they should move right into it.

CATCHING A PASS

Half of any good pass is a good receiver. A good receiver is always creating connections with their teammates. Showing a nice big target helps your teammate know where to pass. If you are moving, you want your target in front of you in the direction you are going so that the pass will meet you when you arrive. Also, when showing a target, you want the ball away from your defender's arms. A great way to make a connection with your teammate is to establish eye contact.

When receiving a pass from a teammate, be ready in a good athletic stance and have your target hand visible. Your arms should be slightly bent and, as the ball is in the air, track it with your eyes. If you are holding off a defender, keep that hold until you are ready to catch.

As you receive the pass, shorten the gap between you and your teammate by stepping to the ball with your arms extended. Try to catch the ball with both hands. This secures the ball if there is any contact from your defender.

As you evolve your catching ability, you will be able to catch bad passes, quick passes or passes with a lot of defensive pressure.

TYPES OF PASSES

PUSH PASS

A push pass is used to get your pass around your own defender as quickly as possible without telegraphing where it is going. The push pass creates a fast, direct line to your teammate. Use it in both the half- and full court to cover distance quickly.

When executing the pass, push the ball directly from your pocket. You pass from your left pockets when passing to the left and right pockets when passing to the right. The pass starts with two hands on the ball in the passing pocket and finishes with one hand pointing in the direction of the pass. You should step toward your target with your same foot as your passing hand in the frontcourt for a shorter, quicker, more powerful pass. Sometimes you will need to step around a defender to make a push pass by extending your arms outside your pockets.

Same Foot, Same Hand

When passing with the same foot, same hand to the right, you push the ball mainly with your right hand while simultaneously stepping with your right foot. Your left hand is still on the ball for protection to allow you to potentially fake a pass. This one-handed release allows for a quick release with a lot of power and speed.

1 The passer is squared up to the basket

2 The passer is in an athletic stance

3 The push pass leaves from her top right pocket

4 The passer steps with the same foot as the passing hand in the direction of the pass because the pass is in the frontcourt

When using a push pass in the full court, more power is needed to cover a longer distance. In this situation, you can use your opposite foot, opposite hand to generate more power.

BOUNCE PASS

Use a bounce pass to pass the ball under the arms of a defender. A bounce pass is a great option when either you or your teammate's defender has their arms up high. You can use the bounce pass when your teammate is cutting into the key, is close to you or has sealed their defender. A bounce pass is a slower pass so it can be easier to catch.

To execute a bounce pass, start with the ball in one of your lower pockets and push it forward and angled toward the floor. The ball should only bounce once before arriving at your teammate. You want the ball to hit the floor about two-thirds of the way to your teammate and bounce directly up to their target hands. If the bounce on your pass is less than the two-thirds of the way, the ball won't have enough distance from the bounce to arrive to your teammate. If the bounce on your bounce pass is more than the two-thirds of the way, the ball will bounce too low, making it difficult to catch. As you play with taller and shorter players, experiment with the distance of the bounce to deliver the best pass. It should be noted that because the bounce pass is slower, quick defenders can sometimes steal it.

OVERHEAD PASS

An overhead pass is used when your defender's hands are low or below shoulder height. You can also use the overhead in the full court to cover longer distances over defenders. If you do not have the strength to cover the distance with a push pass, try using an overhead pass.

When executing an overhead pass, make sure there is an open window at the top of your defender's head. In order to get your defender's hands in this position, you can use a fake. Once their hands are out of the way, bring the ball above your head with your elbows bent. Do not bring the ball behind your head—keep it above so a defender behind you cannot steal it. Use your upper back, shoulders and arms to pass the ball in a direct line from your hands to your teammate's target hands. Your arms will move forward slightly, but a lot of the force comes from snapping your wrists. Take a step in the direction of your pass for longer distances. But remember that the more time the ball spends in the air, the more time the defense has to shift and intercept your pass.

Bounce the ball two-thirds of the distance to your teammate for it to go directly to their target hand.

Good Overhead Pass

1 The passer is in an athletic stance. A poor passer stands upright

2 The passer holds the ball above her head with her arms bent, ready to extend her arms and snap her wrists. A poor passer brings the ball behind their head

FAKING A PASS

Sometimes you want to pass from one of your pockets, but the defender has their hands in the way. If you fake a pass somewhere else, it will often open up the window you are trying to pass through. For example, if you fake a bounce pass or push pass to the defender's lower window, pay attention to their reaction. If the defender's hands move to the lower window to defend your fake, complete a push pass through their upper window. If the defender keeps their hands high, complete a bounce pass or push pass through their lower window. Generally, you want to do one good fake and get a read rather than a series of fakes. Too many fakes will freeze the movement of the ball within the offense.

Elements of good pass fake:
- Stay in your athletic stance
- Sell the fake to get a good read
- Use your eyes to sell the fake

Remember: Fake high, pass low! Fake low, pass high!

PASSING DRILLS

WALL PASSING

Equipment: Wall, ball, tape for targets

Explanation: Use a wall that bounces the ball back to you. Create some targets on the wall with the tape to represent where your teammate's target hand might be. Stand 5 or 6 feet (1.5–1.8 m) from the wall, and practice your one-handed push passes from all four pockets.

Next Steps: Increase the number of passes, the number of targets or the distance from the wall. Add a defender and pass through their passing windows.

Modifications: Try with fewer targets, shorter distances or fewer repetitions.

Variations:

- Change the type of pass you are throwing against the wall to a bounce pass or an overhead pass
- Do no repeat the same pass until all passes have been executed. Try to add in a creative pass that you make up
- Change your stance so that your shoulder is facing the target to simulate a push pass to a teammate around the 3-point line. Make sure to face the other direction so that you practice the pass with the other shoulder facing the target
- Come into your pass off a dribble

 Key Points

Focus on same foot, same hand. Extend your arm and snap your wrists to complete the passes.

20 PASSES:

Equipment: Two to five players, one or two balls, a small space

Explanation: Designate a small space that is the size of the key or the space from the 3-point line to the end line. Complete 20 passes between you and your teammates. Switch the type of pass each time, and, after you pass, move to a new spot. You can do this with up to four teammates.

Next Steps: Emphasize connections before you pass. Use eye contact, target hands and your voice before passing. Let your teammates know if they were missing one of the connections with you to make it a good pass.

Modifications: Use three or more players, add another ball. This makes connections even more important. Change the amount of space designated to vary the distance of passes.

Variations: When you have three, four or five players, add defense and pass fakes. With three players, two are on offense and one is on defense. The offense is trying to complete the 20 passes without a defender intercepting the ball. If they intercept, the passer switches spots with the defense, and the new offense attempts to complete 20 passes. With four players, there can be teams of two on offense and two on defense, or, with five players, have three on offense and two on defense. For an extra challenge, have three on defense and two on offense. Work on adding pivots to your passing to get around the defense.

½ PASSING

Equipment: Half a court, a ball, three players on offense, one or two defenders

Explanation: The defenders choose an offensive player to guard. The offense passes the ball to their teammates if they are one spot away from them. The offense is looking to pass to open players. Once the ball is passed, the passer cuts toward the front of the rim and then exits out to fill a new spot. If there is not a player who is a spot away from the passer, then, upon eye connection, a player who is two or three spots away cuts to fill the one spot away and receive the pass. Defenders must play on-ball defense that is no more than one arm's length away from the passer. After 10 passes, switch the defenders onto offense.

Next Steps: Add a defender for every offense, and work on including fake passes while also working on your connections with your teammates.

Modifications: If the player with the ball does not feel that they can make a safe pass, they can dribble toward a teammate. The player they dribble toward cuts to the rim and then fills an open spot. This gives the offensive team another opportunity to complete a pass. After four complete passes, the offense can look to score.

Variations: You can have the setup with an advantage on offense with three on offense and two on defense. The offensive player who is without a defender cannot look to score but is looking to make a pass to their teammate to score after the five team passes are completed.

6

DEFENSIVE STANCE AND POSITIONS

Defense is important. It might be less glamorous than scoring, but there's no denying the value in stopping your opponent. The more disruptions you make, the harder it is for your opponent to get flow and execute their offense. This gives your team more possessions. Defense requires great effort, and all players can contribute. If you want to make and contribute to a team, pay close attention to this chapter and learn to defend on ball, off ball and in the post with proper footwork and body positioning. Good defensive players rarely come off the court. After all, it is half of every game.

> *"Good basketball always starts with good defense."*
> **BOBBY KNIGHT**

BASIC DEFENSIVE STANCE

A defender's greatest asset is quick footwork. Basic defensive footwork begins with a good athletic stance. Keep your feet shoulder-width apart while in a balanced, seated stance with your knees bent and arms out, taking up space. Your weight should be on the balls of your feet to allow for quick lateral movements. When not moving, your feet should be in a heel-toe distance, where the heel of one foot lines up with the toes of the other. This keeps your stance open and balanced. The quicker your defensive footwork, the more pressure you can apply.

When defending the ball, your forward foot is the foot closest to the side on which the player you're defending is holding the ball. Keep that side's hand in front of you. It is your ball-pressuring hand. Extend it forward, mirroring the ball's movements. Keep your other arm out to the side, taking up as much space as possible to defend the pass.

Keep your stance wide so the offensive player can't get around you. However, if your stance is too wide, you won't be able to quickly move laterally. You need to strengthen your legs to maintain a wide and effective stance. With work, players can have a stance that is much wider than their height might suggest.

You might be tempted to lean your head forward or reach for the ball while in your stance. Only reach if you can maintain your stance. Reaching can put you off balance and slow your reaction speed.

Use a line on the court to measure and feel the heel-toe distance between your feet.

Be sure to keep your heel-toe distance. A stance with a foot too far forward is too open and is easier to get by.

ON-BALL DEFENSE

For an offensive player, there is nothing worse than being challenged by a good on-ball defender. The key to being a good on-ball defender is to apply pressure to the basketball and to keep the player you are guarding contained.

> Containing your player or containing the ball means keeping the player in front of you. You can contain a player in the full court as they bring up the ball or in the half-court as they try to attack the basket.

There are several distances that you can play that influence the level of ball pressure you apply. With practice, you will be able to quickly read the situation and know which distance is called for.

BODY DISTANCE

Body distance is when you are tight to the body of the player you are defending. There is very little space between you and the offensive player.

Reasons to play body distance:

- You want to get the ball out of your player's hands
- Your player is a great shooter
- You are much quicker than your player
- There is very little time left on the shot clock

A risk of body-distance defense is that you are so close to your defender that you may have a hard time recovering if they beat you. Also, at this close a distance, you are vulnerable to committing a foul.

ONE-HAND DISTANCE

One-hand distance is close enough to the defender that you can just reach out your hand and touch them. This distance allows for a good amount of ball pressure. You are also close enough to properly defend a shot. Strong defense is played at one-hand distance.

Reasons to play one-hand distance:

- You are a little quicker than your player
- Your player is a good shooter
- You want strong ball pressure to interrupt the offensive flow

Watch for fouls when playing one-hand distance. Also, focus on your quick footwork to react to your player's movements. At this distance, you might end up out of position or off balance.

> Scoring range is the distance from the basket from which a player can shoot and score consistently. Always be aware of the scoring range of an opponent.

ONE-ARM DISTANCE

One-arm distance gives some space between you and your player while still allowing you to be close enough to apply light ball pressure.

Reasons to play one-arm distance:

- Your player is quicker than you
- Your player has beaten you off the dribble
- Your player is not a strong shooter

There is only minimal ball pressure being applied while playing one-arm distance. If you are guarding a good offensive player, this may not be enough defensive pressure to interrupt their offensive threats. Good players can shoot, attack and score with this amount of space.

GAP DISTANCE

Gap distance puts a significant amount of space between you and your player. It varies, but you are more than an arm's length away. Choose to play gap if you have trouble containing your player, or they are outside their scoring range.

Reasons to play gap defense:

- Your player is much faster than you
- Your player is a poor shooter
- You are focusing on guarding the pass

Without ball pressure, it is easier for the offensive player to see the court and make decisions. A strong shooter cannot be defended from this distance.

> The #1 rule of on-ball defense is to protect the basket by staying between your player and the basket.

ON-BALL SCENARIOS

A JAB STEP

When your player makes a jab step to create space, you need to quickly retreat and recover. In your defensive stance at one-arm distance or closer, your retreat is a two-foot hop. Make sure to keep your heel-toe distance. This retreat gives you space to react to your player's next move and then recover to keep the ball contained.

THE BALL IS ABOVE YOUR PLAYER'S HEAD

When your player lifts the ball above their head, they come out of their athletic stance. This removes their ability to quickly shoot or dribble. Take advantage and close the distance by hopping toward the player with two feet while keeping an athletic stance. Extend one arm straight up to pressure the ball and interrupt a pass. Bend you other arm across your player's chest. With this arm, sense your player's movements and deter them from getting the ball back into a pocket to shoot or dribble. If your player tries to move the ball into a pocket, quickly take a retreat step to recover.

THE DRIBBLE

If your player moves to dribble, beat them to their first step. To keep your balance and maintain your stance, take a quick and long step. The following directions refer to images 1, 2 and 3 at the bottom of the page.

You want to push off with your right foot to allow your left foot to turn in the direction the offense is moving. When lifting your right foot, keep it low to the ground to make the step quick. Reach out with your left arm to help propel yourself left. Stay low and seated with your head up. Don't bring your feet together.

Once your right foot is planted, push off to take a step with your left foot. Keep reaching with your left arm to increase the size of the step.

Keep your head up and your shoulders level. If your player stops, be in the heel-toe stance.

> Keep your ball-pressuring hand on your player's knee to defend a crossover. If your player spins or goes behind their back, do a quick jump to retreat. Always give yourself space to contain.

A DEAD BALL

When a player dribbles the ball, even just once, and picks it up, the ball becomes dead — they cannot dribble again. On defense, you want to capitalize on this opportunity by applying strong body or hand pressure. Your player may pivot to create space. If so, don't reach. Instead, stay in your stance, move and resume strong ball pressure.

OFF-BALL DEFENSE

Even if your player doesn't have the ball, your defensive position is still important. You won't apply ball pressure, but you can still contain your player by staying between them and the basket. You are also responsible for the player with the ball, even though you are not guarding them directly. Always know where that player is and put yourself in a position to always see them. This concept is called guarding one and a half. The "one" is your player, and the "half" is the player with the ball. One and a half is the principle of off-ball defense.

DENY DEFENSE

When your player is one pass away from the offensive player who has the ball, you are in a deny-defense position.

Keys to Good Deny Defense

- In an athletic stance
- Use your peripheral vision to see both your player and the player with the ball
- Turn your hand out to the direction of the ball
- Position yourself about one-quarter of the way on the passing lane

The passing lane is the path the ball must travel to arrive to its recipient. In the image on the opposite page, the two off-ball defenders are using the passing lane to determine where they should be compared to their player. If you are too tight to your defender and not far enough up the passing lane, then your player might cut by you to get the ball. If you are too far up the lane and the ball is thrown over your head, it is too far for you to recover to a good on-ball defensive position.

To know where to be, you need to read the situation and know your opponents. If the player with the ball is a good attacker, play halfway up the passing lane to help your teammate. If the player you are denying is quick, remain at about one-quarter distance to contain them.

Always use your peripheral vision. If you stare at just one player, you leave yourself vulnerable. When you are denying one pass away, you need to be able to see and react quickly to the ball and your player.

HELP-SIDE DEFENSE

When the player you are guarding is more than one passing spot away from the ball, you are in a help-side defensive position. Your role is to protect the basket.

Keys to Good Help-Side Defense

- In an athletic stance
- Guard one and a half
- One third up the passing lane
- Read the court and adjust your position according to personnel
- Communicate with teammates

Help-side defense

Help-side defense

The help-side position is crucial; if your teammate who is guarding the ball gets beat, you are there to rotate and contain their player and protect the basket. This is called being the helper. To guard one and a half from this position, be about a third of the way up the passing lane. Keep your arms out and pointed at both your player and the player who has the ball.

Read the situation and adjust. If you are quick, move further up the pass lane. If your player is a good shooter or a quick attacker, stay closer to them. If the player with the ball keeps getting past their defender, move up the pass lane. In the help-side position, it is important to know the skill sets of your teammates and your opponents.

If you help a teammate who was beat, call out "help!" This lets another teammate know you've left your player and they might need to rotate. This second rotation is called helping the helper.

Don't forget to communicate! The help side is a great position to see what the offense is doing. Call out screens and let your team-mates know if they have help.

TEAM DEFENSE

Team defense requires team-work, communication and adjustments to your individual defensive position depending on the situations and person-nel. But most of all, team defense requires rotations. This is where all the rules of on-ball and off-ball defense come together.

These images show a ball being passed three spots from right to left. Pick a defensive player and study how they rotate from one pass to the next. From what you've learned, are the defensive positions correct as the ball rotates? Based on the positions, what can you read about the skills of the offensive players and the quickness of the defensive players?

Be quick, quick, quick! No matter which position you are in, the quicker you can switch defensive positions, the more you disrupt the offense. Move while the ball is in the air on a pass. Ideally, you will be in a new position the moment an opponent catches the ball.

DEFENSE IN THE POST

When a player is in the post, there are several different defensive techniques and strategies you can use to prevent the ball from being passed to this position. A player with the ball in the post is a huge threat to score, so it is important you take away any easy opportunities. The post defensive positions are modified versions of on-ball, deny and help-side defensive positions.

DENY DEFENSE

When the ball is on the same side of the floor as you or one pass away from the post player you are guarding, you are in a deny defense. The principles of deny defense still apply: an athletic stance, hand in the passing lane and a third of the way up the passing lane.

Keys to Deny Defense in the Post

- Split your player's legs with your defensive stance
- Hand in the passing lane
- Other hand feeling your player's next move
- Ready for on-ball defense

How you deny in the post is determined by where your player is positioned in or around the key and in relation to the ball.

Post Low, Deny High Side

When the ball is on the wing or top spot and the post player is in a position where they are below the halfway mark of the side of the key, you play on the post player's high side. Assume an athletic stance, keeping your hand up and out in the passing lane. Your feet should split your player's inside foot. This ensures that your player cannot easily cut in front or behind you. Keep your other hand on

your player's side. This allows you to feel if they are going to make a move.

> If the player with the ball dribbles toward the baseline, switch from a high-side deny to a low-side deny. Any time the ball is below the post player you are guarding, play on the low side of that player.

Post High, Deny Low Side

If the post player is above the halfway mark on the side of the key, then you play on the post player's low side. The same keys apply to this deny: stay in an athletic stance, split your player's inside foot and keep your deny hand up in the passing lane and your other hand on your player.

> Stay low and balanced in your defensive stance. Get to an on-ball position between the player and the basket. Be ready to move.

HELP-SIDE DEFENSE

When the ball is on the opposite side of the court from the post player you are guarding, then you would take a help-side defensive position. Be in your defensive stance, seeing both your player and the ball. Since your player is closer to the basket, it is important to position your body in the passing lane. If the ball gets to your player in a post spot, it will be a quick and easy score. You might not have much time to recover. Consider this when you decide how far up the passing lane you want to be.

Also, if your player cuts across the key toward the ball side, they are moving into a spot that is one pass away. In this situation, make sure you meet your player early and get into your deny-defense position

Offensive post players are often moving as they cannot have any part of their foot in the key for longer than 3 seconds. As a defender, you will need to readjust as they move and cut to get open. Post defense can look a lot like a dance with your player as you both try to take the advantage.

DEFENSIVE DRILLS

SHADOW DEFENSE

Equipment: Resistance band

Explanation: Imagine you are defending on-ball. Your player has the ball in one of their pockets. Make sure you have your proper heel-toe alignment and arm position. Imagine the player moves the ball and make the proper adjustments quickly.

Next Steps: Imagine the player you are guarding dribbles to the right, move with the dribble and find the proper defensive position. Open your left foot, take one step and use your arm toward your left to contain the ball. Mix that up with drop steps into heel-toe defensive stance and one or two dribbles to get to a position where you are containing the ball. You can have many different combinations: defensive stance, two shuffles to the right, one to the left. Start to move faster, focusing on your form and game speed.

Modifications: Go through the stances slowly and have someone check your key points. Record your movements to see if you are getting all of the key points. Add in a player to move the ball into the pockets and practice your on-ball positions and pressure. They can stop after every offensive movement and give you feedback on your defensive position.

Variations: Add a resistance band over your ankles to start to strengthen your legs and to help work on your speed. Don't do the same pattern of defensive positions every time. Have the imaginary offense switch up their movements.

Key Points

- Make sure you check your form when in on-ball defense:
  - Ball pressure
  - Low defensive stance
  - Heel-toe position

- Big first step on the imaginary dribble

- Game speed

ON-BALL PARTNER

Equipment: Ball, partner

Explanation: One player is on offense with the ball, and one player is on defense. The defense gets into an on-ball defensive stance. The offense moves the ball from one pocket to the other, and the defense reacts and adjusts. The offense lifts the ball above their head, takes one or two dribbles or creates a dead ball situation.

Next Steps: The offensive player adds to the series above with a jab step and spin dribble so that the defense adds in the retreat step. The offensive player can also add a change of direction dribble, going one or two dribbles in one direction before changing.

Modifications: The player on offense can move through the movements, checking the defensive position after each new position. Record the drill to see your positioning. Compare it to the key points.

Variations: After going through three positions, the offense can try to score. If the offense scores, they keep the ball and go to a new spot on the floor. If the offense misses or if the defense steals the ball, then the defense goes on offense.

Key Points

- Focus on the proper defensive adjustments

- Keep your proper form as you work to game speed

- Stay low and balanced at all times

PASSING IN THE KEY

Equipment: Four players, ball, and basket

Explanation: Create teams of two. The offensive team selects a spot on the floor around the perimeter, with one player along the same side of the key. The defense takes the appropriate on-ball and deny-defense positions. The offense can dribble to another spot to move the defense and get a pass into the player in the post spot. The offense can only play on one side of the split line. If the defense gets the rebound, steals or taps it away, they get 1 point and stay on defense. The defenders switch the post spot and perimeter spot on the second possession. If the offense scores, they get to play on defense to earn points. Both teams are trying to get to 10 points. The offense must switch sides of the split line on each possession.

Next Steps: Have your post start on the weak side and then cut across the split line to post up. The defense adjusts to this movement and works to defend the basket and tap or steal the ball.

Modifications: Set up with a passer from a spot along the 3-point line without defense. The post starts on the ball-side low-post spot, and the defender will deny the post. Rotate positions so all players defend. Change to include the high-post spot and a cut from the opposite side. Lower the amount of required points for the defense to three or five.

Variations: Play 2-on-2 live, but only look to shoot if the ball is passed into the post spot first. Defense still gets points if they make a stop and stay on defense. Offense gets to move to defense to earn points if they score.

 Key Points

- Work on your on-ball defensive positioning
- Apply good ball pressure
- Post defense splits the offense's lower foot
- Box out after the shot
- Stay in your defensive stance
- Contain your player
- Communicate with your teammate

STOP-SCORE-STOP

Equipment: Four players, ball, basket

Explanation: Use on-ball and off-ball defensive techniques to stop the other team from scoring. Two players are on offense and fill two spots on the court one with the ball. The two other players match up to the offense in proper defensive positions. Each team wants to get a sequence that starts with a defensive stop and is then followed by a score. The score can be a 2-point or 3-point shot, but it has to be in the next possession. If there is no score in the next position, than that team starts again by working to get another defensive stop.

If they do score in the next possession, then they must get one more stop to win. If there is any interruption, they start again.

Next Steps: Add specific demands to the score. Perhaps it has to include a post entry, a screening action or a front rim cut before scoring. Adding these elements can change how the offense plays and gives different situations for the defense to practice guarding.

Modifications: Shorten the sequence to a stop and a score.

Variations: This drill can be 1-on-1 or 3-on-3. No matter the number, this drill is good practice to learn rotations.

 Key Points

- Communicate with your teammates

- Stay in a low, active defensive stance

- Recognize which type of defense is right for the situation

- Move to your new type of defense on the airtime of the pass

- Choose the distance of your on-ball defense depending on your player's strengths

7

COMBINATIONS

You can pass, dribble and shoot, but, to play better basketball, you need to put these skills together in the right situations. On the court, making good decisions can be as important to success as great skills. Many coaches have benched star players who take difficult shots when their teammate is open for a layup. But decision-making isn't always easy; in a game, you might only have a second to decide what to do. Become a student of the game. This means watching and understanding games and reflecting on the decisions you make in each action. This chapter is not only about combining your skills but also about when to use them. It's about playing with your body and your mind.

> *"Attitude is a choice. What you think you can do, whether positive or negative, confident or scared, will most likely happen."*
>
> **PAT SUMMITT**

TRIPLE-THREAT POSITION

The triple threat is all about having options with the ball. If you stand straight with the ball over your head, you have few options. The defense knows that you have to bring the ball down before you can properly shoot or dribble. These extra movements put you at a disadvantage. But if you are in a triple-threat position, you are ready to pass, shoot or dribble. The defense can't be sure what you are going to do. You are a threat and much more difficult to guard.

Think before you dribble! It can be tempting to do a retreat dribble if your defender is pressuring you, but once you dribble, you can't pick up the ball and dribble again. Keep your options open, and use your dribble with a purpose. Read the defense to make the right decision.

TRIPLE THREAT BASICS

Keys to a good triple-threat position:

- An athletic stance
- The ball is in one of your pockets
- Square to the basket
- Head and eyes are up to see the court
- Ready to shoot, pass or dribble with only a small adjustment

To be in a good triple threat, you must know how to catch the ball. Firstly, catch with your hands as close to a pocket as possible. Remember that, with strong ball pressure, you don't have much time to adjust the ball after the catch. Secondly, catch the ball with a two-foot stop so that you can use either foot as your pivot foot. If you can pivot on either foot, in either direction, you increase your mobility and ability to dribble. On the catch, have your shooting foot (same arm, same foot) slightly ahead of the non-shooting foot so you are also ready for a quick release to shoot.

Practice catching the ball in a triple threat until it is part of your muscle memory. Use a self-toss to practice until your feet naturally get into their shooting position but are also in a position to pivot or move to pass and dribble. If you have

someone who can pass you a ball at different angles, you can pass back and forth and get into that triple-threat position on every catch. The more you practice this, the more natural it will become.

A self-toss is when you toss the ball in front of you with two hands, creating a backward spin so the ball bounces up to set up your catch. Use the self-toss when you are practicing by yourself so you can mimic a pass from a teammate.

DECISION-MAKING

One of the most difficult aspects of a basketball game is knowing when to pass, when to shoot, when to drive and when to dribble. We also often perform these actions together. The options can seem endless, but here are a few things to consider when starting from a stationary offensive position.

> Starting from a stationary position means that you have caught the ball and still have all three offensive options available to you. Starting from a dynamic position is when you are on the move when you catch and flow directly into your offensive options.

TO SHOOT OR NOT TO SHOOT?

If you are in your shooting range, you need to learn when to shoot. You quickly need to read the situation. Where are you on the court? How is your defender defending you? Where are your teammates? Where are the other defenders? If you are within a range from which you consistently score, and your defense is an arm's length or more away from you, you should consider shooting. This distance is important; you have the space you need to get your shot off. Remember to see if one of your teammates has a better shooting option.

Choosing to shoot the ball should be quick, almost automatic. You should make the decision as the ball is being passed to you. How you catch the ball and land with your feet will determine how quickly you can get the shot off before the defense moves to defend you. The quicker you are able to get your shot off when open, the more difficult it is for the defense to defend you. If you take a long time to decide to shoot and get your hands and feet ready, then there is more time for the defense to react and take away your shooting opportunity.

If you are not in your shooting range, your teammates are open or the defense is less than one arm's length away, you want to drive or pass. The quicker you do this, the less time the defense will have to react.

SHOT FAKE AND SHOOT

If you have a defender who is closely guarding you, or you are not sure if you have enough space to get the shot off, consider using a shot fake. If the defense jumps off their feet or stands up out of their athletic stance to defend your fake, you can dribble past them. While they are in the air or out of their stance, pass by them to get a better scoring opportunity or better passing angle to a teammate with a better offensive advantage. If the defender does not move to defend your shot fake or if you feel like you have enough space to get your shot off after your shot fake, you can go right back up and shoot over them.

1 Good triple threat position

2 Starts the shot fake, and the defense doesn't move

3 Defense still does not react to the fake

4 Decides to shoot

> A fake is when you make a move with your head, non-pivot foot, the ball or all three to deceive your opponent and get them to react. Make your movement in one direction to test how the defense reacts. If they react, you can move or execute a skill in a different direction. If the defense does not react to the fake, you can continue in your original direction.

SHOT FAKE, DRIBBLE AND SHOOT OR LAYUP

If the defense is not giving you enough space for your shot, you may want to shot fake and dribble to get by them. If no other defenders rotate to stop you, attack the basket for a layup. If the defense is slow to stop your layup, or the basketball key has defenders in it, then stop your dribble, change your forward momentum to upwards momentum and take your shot.

1 Good triple threat position

2 Shot fake and the defense raises off their feet

3 Dribble past the defender, and decide whether to continue with the layup or make a two-foot jump stop into a shot

SHOT FAKE, DRIBBLE AND/OR PASS

Catch the ball in a triple-threat position, shot fake and, when the defender moves to guard your shot, try to dribble by them to attack the basket. If your defender recovers or help defense takes away your drive, pass to an open teammate. Reading the defense is key to making the right decision. If no help defense comes, then you can continue to attack the basket by finishing at the rim.

1. Good triple threat position

2. Defense puts hand up and lifts their hips on the shot fake

3. Offense attempts to dribble past defender

4. Defense cuts off the dribble

5. Offense passes to open teammate

COMBINATION DRILLS

SELF-TOSS TRIPLE THREAT

Equipment: Ball, chair or cone

Explanation: Self-toss the ball at different angles on the court and practice catching it and getting into the triple-threat position. Once you are comfortable getting into the triple-threat position, self-toss, get into the triple-threat position and complete the following sequence:

1. Shoot as quickly as possible from the triple-threat position while maintaining great form (10 times)
2. Shot fake and dribble directly to the basket and make a layup (10 times)
3. Shot fake, take one dribble and then shoot the ball (10 times)
4. Shot fake, take two dribbles and shoot the ball (10 times)

Next Steps: Do the same drill from different areas on the court, practicing catching from the left and right and attacking to the left and the right. Do a different combination every self-toss.

Modifications: Increase distance from the net. Decrease distance from the net.

Variations: Add a chair or cone as a defender and self-toss the ball at different distances from the chair or cone. Depending on how close you catch the ball from the cone or chair, decide whether to drive or shoot. Keep track of your scores to follow your progress.

Key Points

- Low athletic stance
- Get into triple-threat position with your hands ready and the ball in a lower pocket
- Do not jeopardize form for speed; start slow and increase to game speed

PARTNER PASSING CLOSEOUTS

Equipment: Ball, partner

Explanation: Your partner is under the basket with the ball, and you are moving around the spots on the 3-point line. Your partner passes you the ball and runs out to guard you. Catch the ball in the triple-threat position, and be ready to shoot. If your partner is fast and gets close to you, dribble past them to make a layup. Your partner can pass to you from different distances so you have to make different decisions. Your partner can also change their defensive on-ball distances when they run out to guard you to help you practice different decisions. Once you shoot, get your rebound and finish with a layup if the ball doesn't go in. Now your partner finds a spot on the 3-point line and gets ready to catch the ball. You get the ball and pass to them and go play defense. Continue in different areas of the frontcourt.

Next Steps: Do the same drill from different areas on the court and practice going both left and right.

Modifications: Increase your distance from the net. Decrease your distance from the net. Add another help defender under the basket. If they don't come to help, take the layup. If they come just outside the key, pull up early for your shot.

Key Points

- Low athletic stance
- Get into triple-threat position with the ball in your lower pocket
- Keep head up to read your defense's distances and reactions to your fakes

2-ON-2 COMBINATIONS

Equipment: Ball, four players

Explanation: Two players are on offense, and two players are on defense. The two defenders start under the basket with the ball. The two offensive players are spaced on the 3-point line. The two defenders pass the ball to the offense and then go play defense. The offense catches in a triple-threat position and reads the defense and their teammate. If the defense is quick to get out on the shooter, the shooter may pass to their partner. If the defense is slow, the person who gets the ball shoots. If the person with the ball fakes and drives and the second defender steps in, then they pass to their teammate. This drill will help you practice your combinations and your decision-making.

Next Steps: Switch offense and defense often. Switch who receives the first pass. Use different spots on the 3-point line and start on the left and right sides of the split line.

Modifications: Increase and decrease the distance from the net. Change the starting position of the defense so they are further under the basket, making it a longer distance to defend the first pass.

Variations: This can build nicely to 3-on-3 so that the offense has to read the help defense as well.

Key Points

- Get into triple-threat position, hands ready with the ball in your lower pocket
- Keep head up to read your defense and your teammate(s)
- Reflect with your teammates. Was the best decision made?

8

BOXING OUT

Rebounding requires effort, patience and anticipation. There are two types of rebounds. There are offensive rebounds—a rebound in the frontcourt where you are shooting—and defensive rebounds—in the backcourt where the opponent is shooting. In both cases, you and your teammates are competing for the ball. Boxing out is a technique that will increase your odds of getting possession of the basketball. At all levels of play, rebounding affects the outcome of games. If you are not a great shooter but you can get rebounds, you will always make an impact on the court.

"No rebounds — no rings."
PAT RILEY

Rebounding is about anticipation. It is key to watch where the ball is going and anticipate where it might land. A shot with a low arc may bounce off the front rim and rebound long, whereas a shot with a high arc may bounce around the rim and fall short. By tracking the ball, anticipating its direction, getting there before your opponent and boxing out, you increase your odds of getting a rebound.

HOW TO BOX OUT

The key to a good defensive box out is to go to your opponent and make contact. Many players like to leave their opponent and go straight for the ball. Be patient. First you must find your player, and then you must anticipate where the ball is going to go. Then, you create contact with your player while in a good athletic stance.

1 Off-ball defense is played, and you anticipate a shot

2 A shot is taken. Instead of watching the ball, find your player and make slight contact with your forearm. You have to be careful not to extend your arm and foul your opponent. A slight forearm will ensure you know where they are and want to go. If you hear "shot," the first thing you do is make contact with a player

3 Once you know where your opponent is and in which direction they are going, plant the foot in the direction in which they are starting to move between their feet

4 Once your foot is planted, back pivot into your player to box them out

5 Once you have pivoted, the next step is to seal the offensive player so they cannot get around you. You want to be as wide as you can be. A wide stance with arms up makes it harder for your opponent to get around you. Once you seal your opponent, your eyes should be tracking the ball and looking for where the rebound may go

6 Be in an athletic stance to improve your balance and stability. The opponent is behind you, pushing or moving to get to the ball. When in a strong athletic stance, you have great balance and can shuffle in either direction, so it is hard for your opponent to get around you. You will therefore have more time to see where the ball is going and get there first. With your opponent on your back, they will either foul you by going over your back or give up and retreat

Always box out! Even if your player is not in the play, find someone to make contact with.

If you are trying to get an offensive rebound and are being boxed out, break contact with your player. The more you lean on them, the easier you are to keep in their box out.

BOXING OUT DRILLS

BOX OUT AGAINST A WALL

Equipment: Basketball, wall

Explanation: Place a ball against a wall with one hand. Plant the same foot as the hand that is holding the ball against the wall and back pivot your body, making contact with the ball on your back. The object of the drill is to use a good box out position to prevent the ball from dropping to the ground by maintaining contact and pressing the ball against the wall. Keep your hands up.

Next Steps: Increase your speed.

Modifications: Use a softer ball or find a partner who can hold the ball until you get the idea of back pivoting and holding the ball in place.

Variations: Go in both directions, pivoting around the left and right foot. Hold the ball out to the right or left, making your pivots larger. Pretend a player is trying to get around you and shuffle to the left and the right while keeping your box-out position.

Box out on offense! When a teammate shoots, try to get between your defender and the basket and hold your space with box out techniques.

Key Points

Pivot quickly around and make contact with the ball. With your arms up, keep your stance wide and balanced.

BOX OUT AROUND A BALL ON THE GROUND

Equipment: Partner, basketball

Explanation: Place a basketball on the floor and stand about 4 feet (1.2 m) away. One player faces the ball, and the other player faces that player. The objective for the offensive player on the outside is to touch the ball. The objective for the defensive player on the inside is to box out and keep the offensive player off the ball. When the defensive player says, "Go," the offensive player tries to get the ball. The defensive player plants, pivots and uses a box out. The drill is over if the offensive player cannot reach the ball in four seconds. Switch roles and repeat.

Next Steps: Decrease the distance between the partners and the ball.

Modifications: The defensive player can begin in a deny or help-side stance. The offensive player can incorporate fakes.

> **Safety Tip:** Be careful not to step on the ball when pivoting or shuffling. Place the ball on a roll of masking tape or a coffee lid to prevent it from rolling.

 Key Points

Pivot quickly around and make contact with your partner. With your hands up, keep your partner behind you by anticipating their movements with your body.

9

CUTTING

One of the keys to basketball is getting open, and one of the most effective methods of getting open is cutting. Cutting is a change of speed or direction to move to an open space to receive a pass or create an opportunity for a teammate. There are many different types of cuts in basketball, and which cut you'll use will depend on the defense. Always read what your defender is doing and then make a cut that will give your team an advantage. A great cutter is explosive and can quickly change speed and direction.

"Cutting is so important to great offense. Players need to understand that every cut you make is not always for you. Hard cuts often get others open."

KEVIN EASTMAN

CUTTING BASICS

Make good, strong cuts! Even if you don't get open, selling your cut is important. By making a good cut and bringing your defender with you, you create space for your teammates.

In order to make a good cut there are a few things to keep in mind:

1. Read what your defender is doing. Are they looking away? Is their back turned? Are they tightly guarding you?
2. You want to do the opposite of what the defense is doing. For example, if they are in good deny defense, consider back cutting toward the basket. If they are sagging in the key, consider blast cutting along the 3-point line
3. Set up your defender. You do this by leading the defense in one direction and then, with a quick change of direction and speed, moving in the opposite direction to make the cut
4. When you set up your defender, move at a steady pace. Start to create connections with your teammates to help with the timing of your cut
5. When you go to make the cut, explode off of the foot opposite the direction you want to cut. This creates a quick change of direction and speed
6. When you are cutting, make connections with your teammates. Have a target hand up where you want the pass. Maintain eye contact
7. Timing is critical! You may only have one second to get open. Make sure you are cutting to open space

Great cutters are agile and are able to change direction quickly.

BLAST CUT

A blast cut is when you make a fast, explosive movement in a straight line to receive a pass. Use a blast cut when trying to break pressure in the full court or to move the ball in the half-court. The cut begins with the offensive player standing still or moving slowly and ends with the offense beating their defense to a spot on the floor to receive a pass. This cut works well when the cutter is faster than their defender or their defender is playing gap distance.

1 The off-ball defender is in help defense and is sagging off of her player. The offensive players are too far apart for a successful pass. The cutter makes a connection with her teammate with eye contact

Time your cuts. Only cut after you have made a connection with your teammate.

2 The cutter makes a hard cut in line with the basketball. She cuts to the top spot on the 3-point line that is one pass away from her team-mate. She comes directly to the ball with her target hand showing

Keys to a Blast Cut

• Make a connection with your teammate

• Change your speed suddenly to surprise your defender

• Take a direct path to where you want to catch the ball

BOUNCE-THE-BASELINE CUT

A bounce-the-baseline cut is when you cut away from the ball toward the baseline, plant your foot at or near the baseline and then come back toward the ball while keeping wide on the wing. When going away from the basket, do so at a slower speed, and once you change directions, explode toward the ball.

If your defender follows you, you might open up space at the top of the key for your teammates.

1. The off-ball defender is in a good deny position. It would be hard to get a pass without the defense deflecting it

2. The off-ball player takes her defense away from the ball by running toward the baseline

3. When the cutter gets to the baseline, she plants her lower foot

4. The cutter pauses to make a connection with her team-mate to time her cut

5. The cutter pushes with her baseline foot back toward the wing one-spot away, showing the passer her target hands

This cut is effective due to the change in direction and speed. You need to surprise your defender when exploding back toward the wing.

Keys to a Bounce-the-Baseline Cut

- Stay wide outside of the 3-point line to space out the court

- Time your cut back up to the wing by making a connection with your teammate

- Change your speed at the baseline as you change direction

113

FRONT CUT

A front cut is when the offense moves quickly in front of their defender's side that is closest to the ball and toward the basket or an open space. This type of cut is often effective right after you have passed the ball. Your defender might not have moved or shifted properly into an off-ball deny position.

When doing a front cut, move directly across the face and body of your defender, putting yourself between them and the ball. This cut can often lead to easy baskets by cutting to the front rim with a good target hand. It is also effective when the other team is applying full-court pressure or if your defender turns their head or body away from you.

If you pass the ball and then receive it off a front cut, we call this a give-and-go!

Keys to a front cut

- Read the defense. Can you cut right in front of them or do you need to set them up first?

- Cut tight in front of your defender

- Show where you will need the pass with a target hand

1 The off-ball defender is in a deny position. The cutter sets up the cut by pretending to go behind the defender. A target hand is up to sell the cut

2 When the defender moves below to stop the cut, make a quick change of speed and direction cut in front instead. Connections are made with eye contact and a target hand

Read the court! As a passer, always look to see if help defenders can come to guard the cutter.

115

Front Cut Swim Move

If you are closely guarded, add a swim-arm move to your front cut. Bring your arm that is furthest from the ball up and over the defender to make a good front cut. It can give you a quick advantage on your first step, putting the defense a step behind you. This swim arm becomes your target hand, leading you to the basket. The motion looks like you are doing a front crawl swimming stroke with one of your arms.

1 Ball is passed from the top to the wing

2 The cutter steps in front of the foot of the defender who is closest to the ball. The cutter should get as close as possible and swing their arm furthest from the ball up and over the defender's arm. This seals the defender and gives the cutter a step advantage

3 By staying as close to the defender as possible, the cutter holds the seal so their defender cannot recover

4 The cutter makes connections with the passer. Their swimming arm becomes their target hand. COB your defender

Cut on back, or **"COB,"** is a good concept to understand. When getting by your defender, if you cut on their back and finish your cut movement by putting them on your back, it is very difficult for the defense to recover.

BACK CUT

A back cut is similar to a front cut, but instead of cutting in front of the defense, you cut behind them. A back cut is most effective when a defender is between you and the ball and they turn their head away. Another good use of the back cut is if your defender is over denying you and your eye is lined up with the defender's shoulder. This line up puts you in a great position for a back cut. You can also set your defender up for a back cut. Pretend to cut in front of the defense's face with one step, forcing them to deny your cut. Quickly change directions and speed to cut behind the defense's back. As always, make your connections with the passer.

1 The cutter passes the ball from the top to the wing one space away

2 The defender jumps toward the ball in a strong deny position. Seeing the defender's shoulder, the cutter cuts hard, behind the defender, straight to the basket

3 The cutter has their target hand out, leading toward the basket. As a cutter, don't forget to COB your defender if possible. Make it difficult for them to recover

Keys to a Back Cut

- Read the defense. Can you see the back of your defender's head?

- Set your defender up

- Make connections

- Change of speed

- COB your defender

A back cut is often referred to as cutting backdoor or a backdoor cut

In this photo, see how the defender has turned their head and back to the ball? This allows the passer and cutter to make eye contact. Notice how the cutter also has their target hand out. These are two strong connections being made. From here, the cutter should COB his defender to get an even better advantage.

SEAL TO CATCH

Seal to catch is often used when you are closely guarded and already one space away, close enough for a pass. In this situation, you want to come close to your defender, make contact with them to seal them. Hold the seal and then release the seal to get the pass. This type of cut is often used to inbound the ball, pass into the high or low post and get the ball to a wing that is closely denied.

1 Maintain contact with the defense and hold your wide seal even once the ball has been thrown

2 On the airtime of the pass, explode off your inside leg and release the seal to go to the ball with both hands. Catch in an athletic stance

3 Catch the ball and either get into a triple-threat position, dribble or pivot to create space

Practice your timing. If the defense gets their hand on the ball, then you did not create a seal with your body or you did not hold the seal long enough.

Keys to Sealing to Catch

- Create contact with the passer

- Release your seal to create space to catch

- Hold the seal and extend your target hand

- Release the seal on the airtime of the pass

When sealing, have a wide base so you can maintain the contact and hold your position. Your position to the defender creates a T shape with your bodies. The wider the seal, the harder it is for the defense to get to the pass. Your target hand is an important connection with the seal. The arm that is in contact with the defender should be at a 90-degree angle and should never be extended. It simply protects your space. If you push and extend that arm, you can be called for a foul.

COMBINING CUTS

In an offensive series, athletes and teams often combine different cuts. By working together, multiple players get open so that the passer has more than one option. The more movement and flow, the harder it is for the defense to defend. This maintains good spacing on the floor. If too many players are in the same area, it makes it difficult for the passer to make passes and allows one defender to guard two players at the same time. The key to a good offense is movement and spacing.

One way to combine cuts is called pass, cut, fill. For example, after you pass the ball to a player who has made a cut to get open, make a front or back cut toward the basket depending on the location of your defender. A teammate from the opposite side of the court then makes a cut to fill the position that you vacated.

1 Players are spaced around the perimeter in the wing and two top positions. The ball is in the hands of the middle player in the top left position

2 If the wing player is being guarded, they may need to bounce-the-baseline or seal to catch to receive the pass from the top player. The player at the top of the key makes a push pass to the player on the wing

3 The player at the top pretends to go away from the ball to set up their defender. They then plant their outside foot, change their speed and go back toward the ball to make a front cut on their defender

4 The front cut is made down the key, cutting on their defenders back (COB), making connections with eye contact and by putting a target hand up to tell the passer where to make the pass. At the same time, the other player at the top of the key makes their blast cut to fill the open space one spot away

5 Now the passer has two options for their pass — the first is a front cut toward the basket and the second is a blast cut. This series keeps good spacing and flow

DEFENDING THE CUTTER

CONTROLLING THE CUTTER

We know that the offense is trying to beat the defense to a space to catch the ball. As a defender, you need to find ways to gain an advantage. If a player tries to make a blast cut, the job of the defense is to stay between the passer and their cutter. This requires quick feet, proper positioning, good reactions and active hands. The defense can lead the offense to a place where they do not want to get the ball. This is called "controlling the cutter."

1 The defender is in a good help-side position between the passer and their player. The defense is in an athletic stance with their back to the baseline, protecting the basket. The defense can see both the passer and their player

2 As the offense cuts, the defender meets the player on their cut and beats them to the spot. When defending the cutter, stay between the passer and the cutter. The key is getting the top foot in front of the person cutting

3 The defender is balanced and in an athletic stance, with their feet perpendicular to the offense. Their hand is up and active. The defender sees both the ball and the offensive player that they are guarding at all times

As the on-ball defender, the more pressure you put on your player, the more you help your teammate who is guarding the cutter. Even if the cutter gets open, your pressure might disrupt the pass.

JUMPING TO THE BALL

Any time the player you are defending passes the ball, you want to prevent them from doing a front cut by jumping to the ball on the passing lane. You do this by moving your body closer to the ball so the offense cannot make a front cut. When defending this way, you are allowing the back cut. However, if you keep your eyes on the ball and on your player while keeping a bit of space, you will be in a position to defend the back cut and intercept the ball.

1 The player with the ball passes it to their teammate at the weak-side top position

2 The player defending the passer jumps in the direction the ball is passed. The defender should be moving while the ball is in the air on the pass. The foot closest to the ball leads this jump into the space where the offense would do a front cut, moving the defender toward the ball

3 During the airtime of the pass, the defensive player has moved toward the ball, into a position to prevent a front cut, and is getting ready to deny the pass back to their player

4 Since the defense is in proper position to defend the front cut, the offense makes a back cut. The defensive player continues to stay between the ball and the cutter to prevent the pass to the cutter. While keeping an eye out for the ball, the defense switches their head to face the basket and get a denial hand in the new passing lane to block the possible pass

CUTTING DRILLS

PYLON PLANT AND PUSH DRILLS

Equipment: Pylons or cones

Explanation: Place pylons in a diagonal pattern. The more, the better. Start at one end and plant and push through the pylons. Plant at each pylon to change direction and go toward the other pylons making the motion of a cut.

Next Steps: Increase your speed and vary the distance between the pylons.

Modifications: Decrease your speed and the distance between the pylons. Spread the pylons around a half-court in different spots around the 3-point line. Use different cuts to fill the spaces and cut to the pylons.

Variations: You can bound through the pylons instead of running, which is a type of leap that helps to improve your power and efficiency. You can try to go higher or further with one bound.

Key Points

When changing directions, plant with the foot opposite to the direction you want to go. The body stays in a balanced position, and the arms forcefully swing to provide momentum.

CUTS TO THE BASKET

Equipment: Chair, basketball

Explanation: You can set up a chair to act as a defender. Pass to a partner and practice either cutting in front or behind the chair. Receive the pass back and finish with a layup or different finishes.

Next Steps: Add in a real defender to start to make reads. If the defender jumps toward your pass into denial defense, make a back cut. If the defender stays in the same position, make a front cut.

Variations: Play a game to 7 points with a passer and a defender. While being defended, make a

front or back cut. If you catch the ball, you get 1 point. You get another point if you score. The defense gets a point if they deny your catch.

Key Points

Try to get as close to the chair as possible and COB the chair or guided defender as you pass them. Remember the options to go away from the cut before cutting back in front or behind the chair. Use your change of speed and connections while making your cuts.

SEAL TO GET OPEN

Equipment: Basketball

Explanation: Start on your own in a good position, with your arms wide and in an athletic stance. Lift a target hand and practice leaping with one foot to an open space.

Next Steps: Add a defender on one side and practice getting open without pushing off the arm that is sealing the defender. Make sure to go to the defender to make contact, seal and hold. Finally, add in a passer to work on the timing of the release.

Variations: Play a game to 7 points. If the offensive player catches the ball, they get a point. If the defensive player stops the catch or steals the ball, they get a point. Add a defender on the passer.

Key Points

Open up your seal by having a wide base of support. Hold the seal and extend your target hand. Only release the seal on the airtime of the pass to catch the ball.

10

SCREENS AND PICKS

Working with your teammates increases your chances of scoring. Two important tactics in basketball are screens and picks. Screening is when two offensive players who do not have possession of the ball work together to both get open. Picking is when two offensive players work together, except one player has the ball. While reading this chapter, consider each screen and pick from both the offensive and defensive positions. Decision-making is crucial for effective screens and picks.

"One player can be a crucial ingredient on a team, but one player cannot make a team."

KAREEM ABDUL-JABBAR

SCREENING BASICS

A screen is when one player (called the screener) positions their body to block their teammate's defender. The teammate who receives the screen gets open by cutting to open space. Both players are passing targets. The screener looks to seal, slip or pop after the screen has been used. Two screens are the back screen and the down screen. A back screen is set on the defender's back to get a teammate open closer to the rim. A down screen is set in the direction of the baseline to get a teammate open on the wing or top. There are many types of screens and even screens involving three players.

Seal: The screener opens to the ball, sealing the defense behind them.

Slip: The screener sees that there is no defender between themselves and the basket. With a target hand up, they cut directly toward the basket without completing the screen.

Pop: The screener realizes neither the seal nor slip is open and pops to a new position on the floor to get open.

SETTING THE SCREEN

Only well-set screens are effective. Keys to setting a screen:

1. Find your teammate's defender
2. Run to the space where you want to set the screen, which is in line with your teammate's defender
3. Angle your body so that your back faces the direction you want your teammate to be open
4. Come to a two-foot stop in a low, wide athletic stance. Set your feet so they split the foot of the defender
5. Maintain balance and brace for contact
6. Use your arms to protect your body and create space
7. Hold this position until your teammate uses the screen

If you move too early, this is a foul called an illegal screen. You cannot move to make contact with the defender. If you move, it is a personal foul on you, and your team will lose possession.

USING THE SCREEN

Using the screen is also an important component to an effective screen. How you will use the screen is based on your decisions and reads of your and your teammate's defenders. Keys to using a screen:

1. Be patient and keep good spacing
2. Set up your defense by taking a few steps away from the screen to get a read on the defender
3. Once the screen is set, change your speed and direction and then cut
4. Stay low and balanced and have a target hand up
5. Ensure your shoulder and/or hip are close to the screener's shoulder and/or hip to prevent a defender from slipping in between you
6. Once at the shoulder of the screener, read the defense to decide on your next move

Always remember!

- Both the screener and cutter are scoring options

- The screener and cutter need to work off each other

- Always read the defense

- If one player cuts toward the rim, the other player would pop or space out

READING THE DEFENSE

Down Screen: Defense Switches

Switching is when the defenders exchange who they are guarding as the screen is used. Defensively, you would switch defenders when you are guarding same-sized players, when it is late in the shot clock or the defense is slow to recognize a screen has been set. Offensively, a switch can create a mismatch and, with a good seal, leave the screener open.

① **Offense:** The screener makes a push pass away and prepares to screen

Defense: The defensive players shift to deny and help position

② **Offense:** The screener sets a down screen on the cutter's defender. The screener's back is facing the top spot, where the cutter will be open. The cutter begins to cut to the open spot. The passer on the wing scans the action to see who will be open

Defense: The screener's defender is attached to the screener's hip in a wide stance to prevent a cut or slip to the rim. She shouts "switch" to inform the cutter's defender that they are meant to switch and deny players

③ **Offense:** The passer continues to read who might be open. The cutter cuts to the top spot, trying to beat the new defender there. The screener looks to seal their new defender and then pop out for a pass

Defense: The defender on the screener fights to deny. The cutter's defender quickly gets into a deny position at the top spot or plays on-ball defense if the ball is caught

Down Screen: Defense Goes Under

Going under a screen is when the defense sees the screen coming and steps back to avoid it, going between the screen and the screener's defender. Defensively, you would do this when the person you are defending is a weak shooter or is good at attacking the basket, the screen is set outside of shooting range or you don't want to switch match-ups. Offensively, this can be an advantage because it leaves the person using the screen open for a shot.

1 **Offense:** The screener sets the screen, angling their back to face where the cutter will be open. The cutter cuts to the top spot. The passer scans the action and looks to attack

Defense: The screener's defender calls out the screen, warning their teammate. They are positioned to defend the cutting lane

2 **Offense:** The cutter continues their cut. The screener holds their position in the screen

Defense: The screener's defender steps back, allowing the cutter's defender room to go under the screen

3 **Offense:** The cutter reads that the defense went under the screen. They plant their foot to prepare to shoot on the catch. The screener opens to the play, ready to receive a pass or to rebound

Defense: The cutter's defender tries to quickly recover to on-ball defense, prepares to contest the shot or contains the attack on the basket. The screener's defender plays deny defense on the screener

Down Screen:
Defense Goes Over

Going over a screen is when the defense sees the screen coming and steps to avoid it by going above it. As the screener plants their feet, the defense works to get their inside foot over and above the screener's feet. This type of defense requires good communication and anticipation on the part of the defense. This puts the defender between their player and the screen. Defensively you would use this if the person you are guarding is a good shooter and there is good help defense if the player attacks the basket. Offensively, there is an advantage if the defense is behind you, which leaves a clear path to the basket.

Always be reading your opposition. Anticipation is key to who will get the advantage.

1 **Offense:** The screener sets the screen, angling their back to face where the cutter will be open. The cutter cuts to use the screen. The passer scans the action

Defense: The screener's defender calls out the screen, warning their teammate

2 **Offense:** The screener holds their screen. The cutter reads the defense. Here, the cutter prepares for a pass

Defense: The cutter's defender gets their inside foot above the screener's outside foot. They prepare to cut off the curl to the basket or quickly recover to deny or on-ball defense. The screener's defender stays between the screener and the ball

Down Screen:
Curl to the Basket

If the defense does not get their foot over the screen quick enough, the cutter will make a tight curl toward the basket, leaving their defender behind them.

Offense: The cutter curls toward the basket, hip to hip with the screener, with their target hand up

Defense: The screener's defender must guard two players. They must prevent the screener from slipping and help slow down the cutter on their curl. The cutter's defender must keep track of the cutter and go over the screen, quickly returning to a deny position

When setting a screen, get close to your teammate's defender. The more contact made between you and your teammate's defender, the better your chances of getting your teammate open.

Back Screen:
Defense Goes Over

Back screens are set one step behind the defender's back. The defense on the screener will need to defend both the screener and the cutter momentarily. Communicate that the screen is coming because the cutter's defender won't be able to see.

1 **Offense:** The cutter passes the ball to a player. The screener runs to a spot one step behind the cutter's defender. The screener plants both feet

Defense: The cutter's defender plays deny defense. The screener's defender calls out the screen and plays deny defense

2 **Offense:** The cutter sets up their defender by taking a step in the direction opposite the screen. The screener maintains a balanced screen without moving

Defense: The screener's defender has their hand on the screener's hip, and they are denying the pass. The cutter's defender continues to contain the cutter

3 **Offense:** The cutter quickly changes direction and speed and cuts tight off of the screener's hip. They show a target hand. The screener holds the screen until the cutter has passed and then looks for the pass

Defense: The cutter's defender is caught on the screen. The screener's defender must try to disrupt the cutter while watching the screener

4 **Offense:** The cutter continues their cut toward the basket. The screener cuts to the wing spot. The player with the ball has three options to pass: the cutter, the screener after their screen or the screener after their cut

Defense: The cutter's defender tries to recover to a deny position by going over the screen. The screener's defender gets into deny position and follows the screener on the cut

Call it out. Communicate with your teammate that a screen is coming and how you are going to defend it.

SCREENING DRILL

TWO-BALL SCREENING

Equipment: Two balls, four players

Explanation: Have two players at the top spot with a ball each (Players 3 and 4), one at the top spot without a ball (Player 2) and one on the wing without a ball (Player 1). Player 2 sets a down screen on Player 1's imaginary defender. Player 1 curls tight to the screen. Player 3 passes to Player 1, and Player 1 continues to the basket to score a layup. Once Player 1 has passed the screen, Player 2 uses a back pivot to seal and look for a pass coming from Player 4 for a shot. Repeat three times and switch spots.

Next Steps: Try different options and screens. Use both down screens and back screens. Have the cutter and screener curl, slip and pop to the top spot and the wings. Change the location of the screen and where the pass is coming from. There are many combinations you can practice.

Modifications: Use one ball instead of two. Have Players 1 and 2 do a different screen and read every time. Add a defender or two and have players read the defense to decide their cuts and reads. Include both the right and left sides of the court.

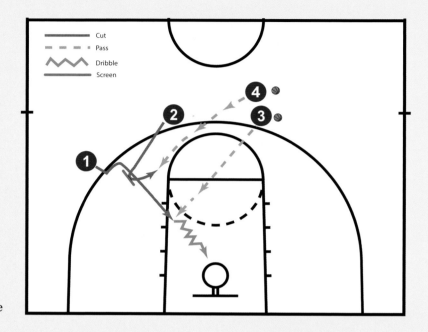

———	Cut
– – –	Pass
∿∿∿	Dribble
——	Screen

Key Points

- Set up the defender to use the screen

- Screen where the defender would be

- When using the screen, come shoulder to shoulder or hip to hip

- Ensure pass is on time and on target

- Be balanced and ready to catch and score quickly

PICKING BASICS

Picks are used to get a player with the ball open. The screener positions their body to block their teammate's defender. The player with the ball uses their dribble and the pick to create space for them to shoot, drive toward the basket or pass. Picks can be used all over the basketball court.

Use a pick late in a shot clock to release ball pressure on a teammate. As you advance, you can use double picks or even combine a screen and a pick.

SETTING THE PICK

Keys to setting a pick:
1. Find your teammate's defender
2. Cut to where you want to set the pick
3. Position your chest perpendicular to the defender's shoulders, angling your back to where your teammate will go
4. Come to a two-foot stop close to the defender in a low, wide athletic stance
5. Use your arms to protect your body
6. Hold this position until your teammate uses the pick. If you move, it is a foul

USING THE PICK

Using the pick requires patience, reading the defense and decision-making. Keys to using a pick:

1. Wait for the pick
2. Once the pick is set, fake one direction and then dribble in the other direction
3. Lead your defender into the pick, staying tight to it
4. Read the defense and decide whether to shoot, drive to the basket or pass

TOP PICK: DEFENSE SWITCHES

1 **Offense:** The picker sets the pick. He is in a low athletic stance with arms protecting the body to create space. The dribbler sets up the pick by moving away and then changing directions

Defense: The picker's defender calls the pick and keeps one hand on the picker to prevent a slip. The dribbler's defender plays on-ball defense and prevents his player from rejecting the pick

2 **Offense:** The dribbler uses the pick, passing the picker tight, and tries to attack the basket. The picker maintains the pick until the dribbler has passed. Then he back pivots into a seal

Defense: The defenders switch. The picker's defender takes a large step to contain the dribbler. The dribbler's defender jumps behind the picker to quickly get into a deny position

TOP PICK: DEFENSE GETS CAUGHT

If the dribbler's defender does not jump behind the picker to a deny position, this allows the picker to back pivot to a seal.

1 The dribbler's defender gets stuck on the pick and is late getting into a deny position

2 The picker back pivots and seals. The dribbler creates space

3 From a wide, low stance, the picker shows a target hand. The picker maintains separation by keeping their other arm at a 90-degree angle

TOP PICK: DEFENSE GOES UNDER

1 The pick is set

2 **Offense:** The dribbler uses the pick by getting to the picker's hip. The picker maintains the pick until the dribbler passes

Defense: The picker's defender steps back to make space between themselves and the pick. The dribbler's defender steps back and through the space created. They look to meet the dribbler on the other side of the pick in good on-ball defense

3 **Offense:** The dribbler reads the defense. He decides to cross back over, using the picker as a shield for an open shot

Defense: Both defenders get their hands up to contest the shot and box out

TOP PICK: DEFENSE GOES OVER

1 The pick is set

2 **Offense:** The dribbler uses the pick. The picker maintains the pick until passed

Defense: The dribbler's defender gets their inside foot over the top of the pick, not getting caught. They recover to good on-ball defense

3 Having got over the pick, the dribbler's defender has neutralized any advantage from the pick

4 The offense can create another advantage by re-picking after the dribbler crosses back over. The second pick is difficult to defend and requires communication and effort to recover

TOP PICK: DEFENSE TRAPS

1 The dribbler's defender fights over the pick. They make sure the dribbler cannot cross back over. The picker's defender keeps their hand on the picker's hip while taking an on-ball stance to contain the dribbler

2 Together, both defenders form an L-shape to surround the dribbler. The L-shape begins with their feet, leaving no space. The goal is to both contain the dribbler and keep them from escaping

3 The dribbler looks to split the trap by finding space between the trappers' feet to attack or pass

4 If the defenders' arms are down, a pass can be made over and out of the trap

There are many ways to guard screens and picks. This chapter covered a few.

PICKING DRILLS

CHAIR PICKS

Equipment: Ball, chair, basket
Explanation: Place a chair at one of the perimeter spots around the 3-point line, which will act as your teammate who is setting a pick. Use the chair to practice your footwork for picks and shot opportunities, both rim attack and shots. Make sure to cover both your defender going over and under the pick.
Next Steps: Replace the chair with a partner who can be a live player setting the picks, as well as a pass option. Add in a player to defend you or the person setting the pick. Switch your role in the drill to try all roles.
Modifications: Call out what the defense is doing and what your read is. For example: "Going over!" and "Attack the basket!"
Variations: Move the chair. Go both left and right on the pick. Add multiple chairs, and try to use different footwork and shots at each chair in sequence.

DEFENSE'S CHOICE

Equipment: Four players, ball, basket
Explanation: Create two teams of two. The defensive team decides whether they will switch, trap or go over or under. One player passes the ball to their teammate to start the drill and then sets a pick on their defender. The defenders then defend and the offense looks to score. If the offense scores, they get 1 point.
Next Steps: Add an offensive passing option. They are there if the offense is unable to get anything off of a pick. Pass them the ball and then reset.
Modifications: Have the defense repeat one defensive method. Once comfortable, add a second type of defense. The defense can play at different defensive pressures.
Variations: Set the picks at various locations on the floor. Start the drill from the opposite free-throw line or an out-of-bounds situation.

PICKING 2-ON-2

Equipment: Four players, ball, basket
Explanation: Play 2-on-2, looking to score. You can only count points coming off the pick or passing to the picker.
Next Steps: Keep score. First team to 10 wins.
Modifications: Say what the defense is doing and then say your read.
Variations: Start the ball in the backcourt, from an inbounding situation or at a different spot on the floor.

 Key Points

- Watch your spacing
- Combine cuts and picks
- Reset if the pick fails
- Is the picker open?
- Read the defense
- As the picker, pivot and seal to create opportunities

 Key Points

- Set up your defender
- Get close to the pick
- Attack the rim in a direct line
- Imagine the defenders

 Key Points

- Good communication
- Offense:
  · Keep your head up
  · Read the defense
  · Set strong picks
- Defense
  · Call the picks
  · Anticipate the pick

11

1-ON-1

1-on-1 is the ability to read your defender and beat them to an open space while gaining an advantage. You can use 1-on-1 skills in the driveway against a friend, in the half-court playing 3-on-3 or on a team in a full game. Bringing your 1-on-1 skills to a team allows you to fully contribute to its offensive system. There are three different types of 1-on-1: dynamic, static and live. Having dynamic, static and live 1-on-1 skills in your game allows you to punish the defense with your counter moves. In this chapter, we break down dynamic and static 1-on-1.

"You cannot achieve unless you believe in yourself. You are more capable than you think."

ELENA DELLE DONNE

DYNAMIC 1-ON-1

Dynamic 1-on-1 is when you create an advantage by catching the ball while cutting. Here, you read your defense on your cut so that, on your catch, you can immediately react. This works well on every cut and is difficult to guard. It forces all defenders to guard cuts, which distracts them from being able to help. Dynamic 1-on-1 takes time to learn, as the read occurs on the move of the cut. We will go through several of the reads and what you should see in order to make your next decision to create your advantage.

Keys to Dynamic 1-on-1:

- Move prior to the catch to activate the defense

- Read your defender before you catch and react

- Catch the ball in a spot that is one pass away from the passer

A **lateral stop** preserves your speed when you want to quickly turn back in the direction you came from. With your knees bent, keep most of your weight on the foot closest to where you came from, so that your other foot is free to quickly crossover in the new direction.

DEFENSE TRAILS, YOU CURL

1 Start on the wing. Your defender should be playing help-side defense, head angled to see both you and the ball. Set up your defender by planting your foot toward the baseline to burst off in the opposite direction

2 Make a blast cut to fill the top spot. As you cut, look over your shoulder at your defender. If they are trailing, prepare to curl toward the key on your catch. Have your target hand up to connect with the passer. Plant your outside foot as you catch

3 After the catch, plant your inside foot to curl around your trailing defender and dribble the ball. A good, tight curl will put your defender on your back

4 Don't forget to COB. This will allow you to dribble into your defender's path and stop them from recovering

DEFENSE PLAYS HIGH, YOU CROSSOVER

1 After making your blast cut away from the baseline, read your defender's position. If your defender is not trailing but is instead high, prepare to crossover on the catch

2 Catch the ball with a lateral stop, putting your weight on your outside foot and the ball in your lower right pocket

3 Quickly take your inside foot and cross it over toward the baseline. Rip the ball low across your body and dribble. Stay low and balanced. Be prepared to take contact

4 Try to plant your inside foot beside or past your defender's feet. This will establish a good COB position and is why proper weight distribution on the catch is so important. Push the ball out and away from the defender on the dribble

5 With proper COB, there should be a clear path to the basket. Stay low and be prepared for contact as your defender tries to recover

DEFENSE GAPS, YOU SHOOT

1 Set up your defender to make a cut to the top spot. Keep your head up and your eyes on the ball

2 Make a quick blast cut to the top spot. Over your shoulder, read your defender as you cut. If there is a large gap, be prepared to catch and shoot

3 Catch the ball in a pocket, ready to shoot. Come to a 1–2 stop or a two-foot stop to quickly establish your shooting position

4 With the space, take your uncontested shot as your defender tries to recover

Shoot your shot! Decide to shoot as the pass is in the air. Reading your defense is important.

DEFENSE CONTAINS, YOU TRIPLE THREAT

1 Connect with your passer and blast cut to the top spot

2 As you cut, read your defender over your shoulder. They are in a good defensive position if they are not ahead, trailing or gapping

3 If your defender contains you on the catch, go into a triple threat. Your options are to pass to an open teammate or use a static 1-on-1 move to create an advantage

If the defense denies your catch, back cut. It is difficult for a defender to deny your catch and then guard your back cut. If you do this once or twice, your defender will likely expect the back cut.

STATIC 1-ON-1

Static 1-on-1 happens after you receive the ball and are contained by your defender. From a triple-threat position, use a jab, a shot fake or a combination to get a read from the defender and create your advantage. Static 1-on-1 is used in a mismatch or isolation situation or if the ball has been frozen and your team's offensive movement has broken down. It can also be effective in transition or late in the shot clock. It is ideal when the ball has come off of movement and the help defense has not already rotated. If you go to static 1-on-1 too early and too often, your team will have difficulty finding offensive flow.

Keys to Static 1-on-1

- Maintain an athletic stance
- Know your pivot foot
- Jab your non-pivot foot
- Read the defense carefully
- Be patient but don't hold the ball too long

A **jab step** is when you test your defender and get a read to create your static 1-on-1 advantage. While keeping most of your body weight on your pivot foot, step your non-pivot foot toward your defender. A light, quick jab step gives you a good read.

JAB AND SHOOT

1 After the catch, get in a triple-threat position. The defender is in a good on-ball defensive stance

2 Jab aggressively at your defender with your non-pivot foot. The defender reacts by retreating. Remember to keep your weight on your pivot foot

3 After you read your defender, bring your jab foot back into a shooting stance. While you do this, quickly get the ball into your shooting pocket

4 Convert your momentum up and take your shot. Recognize how much space and time you need to get your shot off uncontested

JAB AND CROSS

1 After the catch, get in a triple-threat position. The defender is in a good on-ball defensive stance

2 Jab toward your defender. Read your defender and note if they move their inside foot and body toward the jab, intending to stop your drive

3 Lift your jab foot and cross it to the outside of your defender. A light and balanced jab foot can move quickly. Place this cross step beside or past your defender. Stay low and balanced, so you can absorb contact from your defender

A **mismatch** is when an offensive and defensive player are matched up and there is a distinct difference in skill, height, strength or athletic ability between the two.

Isolation is when an offensive player and their defender are in the half-court and have been given a lot of space, usually one or two open spots, to go 1-on-1.

JAB AND GO

1. After the catch, get in a triple threat with the ball in a lower pocket. Here, the defender is in a good on-ball defensive stance

2. Jab at your defender, keeping your stance and balance. Read if your defender does not react to your jab

3. With your weight on your pivot foot, you can now take a quick step around your defender

with your jab foot. Maximize your advantage by not bringing your jab foot back and stepping beside or past your defender. The quicker you make that first step after the jab, the harder it is for the defense to react.

4. Put the ball out front and away from the defender. If your defender tries to recover, remember to COB

LIVE 1-ON-1

THE SHOT FAKE

In static 1-on-1, you get your defensive player to move so that you can make a decision based on a read. In chapter 7, we introduced a shot fake that also gives you a read. The footwork is very similar to the jab step move. Add the shot fake to your static 1-on-1, giving you three more reads and moves:

- Shot fake to a shot
- Shot fake and go
- Shot fake and cross

Make your shot fake from a triple-threat position. From there, if the defender jumps up, take your non-pivot foot and go to the rim or cross your non-pivot foot past the defender.

When making your go or cross step after your shot fake, you still want to stay low, get your first step at the level or past your defender and COB. If you do your shot fake and your defender does not react, then you could go back up for a shot.

Sometimes to get a good read you may have to jab twice in a row. Other times you might jab and then shot fake. The better you sell your shot fake or jab step, the easier you will be able to read your defender and decide on your next move.

Live 1-on-1 is when you have already begun your dribble. This often occurs in transition, during a press break, coming off a pick action or when you start your dribble on your catch. The challenge with live 1-on-1 is that, if you dribble, you forfeit your triple threat, decreasing your opportunities. To be most effective in live 1-on-1, you need strong dribbling skills with both hands. Live 1-on-1 is difficult to guard, as you can be unpredictable when you are already moving.

The strongest scoring threats combine dynamic, live and static 1-on-1 moves. With these tools, you will be better able to read and react to your defender.

1-ON-1 DRILLS

DYNAMIC 1-ON-1 FOOTWORK

Equipment: Four cones, ball, basket, three players

Explanation: Set up two cones about 2 feet (60 cm) apart on the left and right wings of the court. One offensive player has the ball in the top spot and another offensive player starts in the corner on the same side of the court. A third player defends the player in the corner in a help-defensive position. The player in the corner cuts to the wing spot for the pass. The defensive player must run around the outside pylon and chase the offensive player or run and touch the inside pylon. The player that is cutting to the wing spot should read their defense before the catch to see if they are going around the outside pylon or running to touch the inside pylon.

On the offensive player's catch, if the defense goes around the outside pylon and trails the offense, then they should curl and attack the basket. On the offensive player's catch, if the defense touches the inside pylon, then the offensive player should cross and attack the basket. The ball should be passed back out to the player in the top position and the players should repeat the actions and decisions on the other side of the court. Once the offense has caught the ball on both sides and attacked the basket, players change positions so that everyone has the opportunity to be passer, cutter and defender.

Next Steps: Have the defense play either gap, deny or on-ball defense. Move the cones to new spots on the floor.

Modifications: When practicing a specific read, have the defender show the same read a few times in a row. This can help you get used to seeing what the read looks like and focus on the form of your offensive movements. Start with the one read and work through into the cross step and the gap.

Variations: Add a help defender on the attack and decide whether to finish with a layup or pull up for a shot. Add an offensive player on the opposite wing, to add a player attacking to finish with a pass to their teammate on the wing.

Key Points

- Read your defense before your catch

- Use the two-foot lateral stop and cross if the defense goes to touch the inside pylon

- Use the inside foot to a curl if the defense goes over the outside pylon

STATIC 1-ON-1 TRAIN

Equipment: Ball, basket

Explanation: Two players start in a tandem train set up under the basket with the top player holding the ball. The top player tosses the ball out to a spot on the 3-point line and runs after the toss. As they catch the ball, they pivot to square up to the basket. The second player chases and plays on-ball defense. The player with the ball uses their static 1-on-1 skills and reads to score, and the defender tries to stop the offense from scoring. Make sure that when the offense tosses the ball they sometimes use their left pivot foot and sometimes they use their right pivot foot. After the result of that possession, both players switch roles and reset under the basketball and start again to another spot.

Next Steps: Add a 3- to 5-second time restriction. Make it competitive by keeping score between the players. Each player gets five tosses, and if they make the correct static 1-on-1 read, they get a point. If they score, they get a second point. The player with the most points after five tosses each wins.

Modifications: The offense works on the read of one or two of the static 1-on-1 skills at a time. You can add in a third read so that the defense jumps to the jab step and the offense crosses and goes. If your shooting range is not at the 3-point line, make the tosses to spots inside the 3-point line.

Variations: Add a third player to the train before the toss as a second offensive player. When the ball is tossed out from the first player, the second player follows and plays defense, and the third player finds another spot on the perimeter. If the offense can't get a read before the 3–5 seconds, they pass the ball to the other offensive player and cut to a new spot to get the ball back for another chance to do their static 1-on-1. A third player can also act as a second defender. When the ball is tossed out from the first player, the second player follows to play defense, and the third player stays as help defense under the basket.

Key Points

- Sell your moves to get a good read
- Don't drag your pivot foot
- Work on using both pivot feet
- Take your time on your read and react quickly

2-ON-2 TRAIN

Equipment: Ball, basket, timer

Explanation: Four players stack in a train formation under the basket. Their order is Offense 1, Defender 1, Offense 2 and Defender 2. Offense 1 has the ball and tosses it out to a spot on the 3-point line. Defender 1 follows and plays on-ball defense. Offense 2 runs out to a spot on the 3-point line, and Defender 2 follows to play off-ball defense. The offensive players use their dynamic and static 1-on-1 skills to score. They can cut and pass the ball until they find a good opportunity. Once the offense scores or the defense stops them from scoring, the train sets up again and the players switch roles.

Next Steps: Use your partner on your attacks to pass the ball back out if you do not get a good first look on the attack. Put a 24-second timer on to mimic the 24-second shot clock. If the ball touches the rim, reset to 14. You can also set the clock to 14 seconds to mimic the shot clock that occurs in different situations during the game.

Modifications: If the players are struggling, you can create a rule that both offensive players have to touch the ball before the team can score. Have the defense play different distances of on-ball defense.

Variations: For more flow, when the defense stops the offense from scoring, keep playing until a team gets a score-stop-score consecutively. Once that occurs, reset the train under the hoop, switching the offense and defense. That series of a score-stop-score would consist as 1 point. Play first team to 3 points.

Key Points

- Make sure passes are one spot away
- Use both dynamic and static 1-on-1 moves
- Use reads. Don't just rely on speed
- Don't allow the defense to gap in this drill

12

STRENGTH AND AGILITY TRAINING

Basketball requires strength, agility, speed and power. In order to set yourself above other players, you need to put time into not only practicing individual skills but also training your body. Strength helps you protect the ball and seal during a box out. Increased agility leads to more effective cuts. With speed, you will contain your player on defense and beat your player on offense. Power is important for jump balls, rebounds and changes of direction. Developing skills is only one part of the equation. The more you train your body, the more impact you will have on the court.

"You have to not only love the game, you have to love the training, the practice and the competing."

MAYA MOORE

STRENGTH EXERCISE BASICS

When performing strength exercises, form is important. Proper form ensures that you don't get hurt and that you are building the correct muscles. When thinking of form, try to have an athletic stance at all times. You always want to feel balanced. You want your body to be aligned from your feet to the top of your head. You want your hips to be level. Your knees should never go over your toes, and your shoulders should be rounded and back. This starting position ensures you are properly aligned. When doing strength exercises, never sway. Start with lighter weights to establish a correct form. Move slowly and steadily to ensure your muscles are using as great a range of motion as possible.

Remember!

1. Athletic stance
2. Slow and steady movement
3. Use entire range of movement
4. Form over weight
5. Breathe while lifting

KEY EXERCISES FOR BASKETBALL

Definitions

Strength: The amount of weight you can lift with a muscle contraction while maintaining proper form.

Power: The ability to generate as much force as fast as possible.

Agility: The ability to change direction quickly.

Speed: The ability to move as quickly as possible.

Form: A way to safely execute an exercise using the right movement patterns while isolating the intended muscles.

Plyometric: Plyometric exercises exert maximum force in as short a period of time as possible, typically using body weight. Plyometric exercises build power, which is needed in basketball.

Flexibility: Being able to move a muscle through as great a range of motion as possible. The greater your range of motion, the more of your muscle you are training.

Repetitions: The number of times you perform the exercise. For example, you may complete 10 sit-ups. That would be 10 repetitions or "reps" for short.

Sets: The number of times you repeat your repetitions. For example, you may do 10 reps of sit-ups three times. This is three sets of sit-ups.

Warm-up: Before beginning a program, you must always warm-up the muscles you are working. This can be done by riding a bike or running at about 50–60 percent for 5 to 15 minutes.

Cool-Down: Cool-down is done at the end of a program to decrease your heart rate, ensure your muscles are relaxed and reduce muscle soreness by getting rid of any lactic acid that may be built up in the muscles.

MOUNTAIN CLIMBERS

Develops: Core strength to help with balance, defense, passing and shooting.

Equipment: Basketball

Explanation: Put both hands on the basketball and make a plank with both feet extended from the ground. Keep your body straight. Stay balanced with your hips facing the ground, lift one knee toward your chest without moving your arms or rotating your hips. Extend your leg back into a plank. Repeat with the other leg.

Modifications: If stabilizing on a basketball is too difficult, remove the basketball and put both hands on the ground, shoulder width apart. Decrease reps and sets to make it easier; increase reps and sets to make it more difficult. Add a push-up.

 Key Points

- Use your core to lift your legs to your chest

- Try to minimize any other movements

- Hips should not be hinged

- Hips should be parallel to the floor

OBLIQUE V-SIT

Develops: Core strength (specifically oblique muscles) to help with balance, layups, shooting, defense and passing.

Equipment: Basketball

Explanation: From a V-sit position with legs extended in the air at a 45-degree angle, start with the ball on one side of your body. Using your oblique stomach muscles, twist your torso and move the ball to the opposite side of the body and return it back to the original starting position.

Modifications: Put your feet flat on the ground to make it easier. Use a lighter ball or object to make it easier. To make the exercise harder, lower your legs but keep them just off the ground. You can also extend your arms and lift the ball over your head when moving it side to side.

 Key Points

- Maintain a strong core

- Keep the upper body and legs as still as possible

- Use the core muscles to twist the torso

- Lead with the core and not the shoulders

- Tap the ball down beside the hips each time the ball goes from side to side

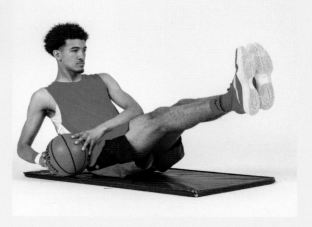

BASKETBALL SQUAT

Develops: Strength of quadriceps and hamstrings, which helps with jumping, needed for rebounds, change of speed, jump balls and defensive stance.

Equipment: Basketball

Explanation: Hold the basketball at chest height. Bend your legs while sitting back so your knees are at 90 degrees. Extend your legs to their original position.

Modifications: Hold basketball out, with arms extended. Use a medicine ball instead of a basketball. To make it easier, do not bend all the way to 90 degrees. Hold the ball with your elbows out to the side and under your chin to include work on rebounding arm position. To combine muscle work, add a torso twist at the bottom of the squat, or move the ball above your head during the extension.

 Key Points

- Feet shoulder width apart
- Ensure knees do not go over toes
- Knees bent to 90 degrees
- Feet stay planted evenly on the floor

171

BASKETBALL SQUAT JUMP

Develops: Power and strength used for rebounds, defense and the jump ball.

Equipment: Basketball

Explanation: Complete a squat by bending your knees to 90 degrees while sitting back. At the bottom of the squat, push off the ground and explode into the air bringing the ball high above your head. Land by absorbing the force in an athletic position. Repeat.

Modifications: Alter the height of the jump. Do not use a basketball or medicine ball to start. Add jumping over a line side to side or front to back.

 Key Points

- Feet shoulder width apart
- Knees bent to 90 degrees
- Explode off the ground
- Ball high in the air
- Absorb landing prior to bending knees again
- Ensure knees to do not go over toes

BASKETBALL LUNGE TWIST

Develops: Core, quadriceps and hamstrings, which are important for defense, cuts and rebounds.

Equipment: Basketball

Explanation: Step forward with one leg while keeping your back knee bent. While in the lunge position, twist to one side and back to the middle. Return to the middle, step back and stand up. Repeat with the other leg.

Modifications: Alter the height of your lunge. Alter how much you twist. Add a medicine ball. Extend your arms. Lunge at 45-degree angles or backward into the lunge twist.

 Key Points

- Keep knees forward
- Ensure knees do not go over toes
- Keep hips forward
- Lead with the torso and not the shoulders or hips
- Keep elbows high. Chin the ball
- Knees bend at 90 degrees

BOX JUMP

Develops: Power, rebounds and shooting.

Equipment: Basketball, box

Explanation: Swing your arms and explode up onto the box. Balance on the box and jump down on the other side. Repeat going back up on the box, without bouncing.

Modifications: Alter the height of the box. Begin with smaller boxes and progress to higher boxes to generate more power.

Key Points

- Swing arms

- Try not to bounce on the jump

- Land squarely on the box with bent knees

- Absorb landing by bending knees when jumping off the box

- Safety is important. Do not jump higher than your ability, and make sure the box is stable

CONE JUMPS

Develops: Agility for cuts, screens and dribbling.

Equipment: Cones

Explanation: Set five to six cones up so that they are on a 45-degree angle from each other. Starting at one end, run to the first cone, plant the foot closest to the cone and explode and run to the next cone. Once at the next cone, plant the foot closest to the cone and explode to run to the next cone. Continue building up to game speed.

Modifications: Increase and decrease the number of cones. Increase and decrease the distance between the cones. Add a basketball and practice various change-of-direction dribbling moves when you plant your foot.

 Key Points

- Plant the foot that is closest to the cone

- Swing the hand opposite to the foot that is planting to generate maximum force

- Keep eyes and head up

- Keep a low athletic stance throughout

- Ensure knees never go over toes

BOUNDING

Develops: Agility and power for cuts, screens and defense. Great to help prevent ankle and knee injuries.

Equipment: Cones

Explanation: Plant foot near cone and explode to the next cone diagonally in front by bounding instead of running. Bounding is the action of leaping. Cones should be close enough together so that you can leap from one cone to the next.

Modifications: Increase distance between cones. Bound backward through the diagonal cones. Switch feet. Add a ball.

Key Points

- Opposite arm and opposite foot
- Knee over ankle and not over toes
- Balanced body
- Weight on foot closest to the cone
- Control landing to absorb force and maintain ankle and knee stability
- Gain and maintain balance prior to bounding to the next cone

ONE-FOOT CONE JUMPS

Develops: Power, one-foot takeoffs and ankle stability.

Equipment: Cones

Explanation: Jump over a cone by taking off on one foot and landing on the other side on the same foot. Switch feet.

Modifications: Use different sizes of cones. Try to jump either diagonally frontward or backward over the cone.

🏀 Key Points

- Swing arms to generate force
- Drive knee high
- Push off the ground with foot
- Absorb landing

TWO-FOOT CONE JUMPS

Develops: Power and jumping for rebounding and defense.

Equipment: Cones

Explanation: Swing your arms and jump over the cone, landing on the other side. Take off and land on two feet.

Modifications: Use various sizes of cones. Try to jump either diagonally frontward or backward over the cone.

 Key Points

- Bend legs
- Swing arms
- Explode off the ground
- Absorb landing
- Takeoff and land with equal weight on both feet

TRICEPS DIP

Develops: Triceps help increase shooting range, boxing out and rebounding.

Equipment: Bench, chair or box

Explanation: With hands on bench or box behind you, stretch out your feet and bend your arms to 90 degrees, working the back of your arms. When your arms are bent at 90 degrees, push back up to the starting position.

Modifications: Alter the height of the box (the lower the height, the easier the exercise will be). You can bend your knees and place your feet flat on the ground.

 Key Points

- Body is straight

- Hips are not hinged

- Arm bend does not go beyond 90 degrees

- Head is up

- Shoulders are back

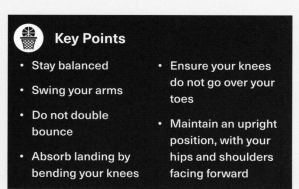

TWO-FOOT DOT DRILL

Develops: Agility and power for offensive moves and one-foot takeoffs.

Equipment: Dots or marks on the ground

Explanation: Arrange five dots like the face on a die. Start in one corner and jump off two feet to the center dot. Land without bouncing. Then jump to another dot.

Modifications: Change the order in which you jump on the dots. Increase or decrease the distance between the dots. Time yourself while keeping good form. Change directions. Switch to one-foot jumps.

Key Points

- Stay balanced

- Swing your arms

- Do not double bounce

- Absorb landing by bending your knees

- Ensure your knees do not go over your toes

- Maintain an upright position, with your hips and shoulders facing forward

AGILITY LADDER

Develops: Agility, footwork and a quick first step on offense.

Equipment: Agility ladder, skipping rope or chalk

Explanation: There are many different footwork combinations you can perform using an agility ladder. The idea is to repeat the pattern of footwork over the entire ladder as quickly as possible.

Modifications: Use different combinations or make up your own combination. Try to go faster, adding in more repetitions and sets. Go through the ladder backward using the same footwork. Add a ball and perform the footwork while dribbling. To activate your core, add holding a basketball in front of you or above your head.

 Key Points

- Maintain balance and athletic stance
- Head and eyes up
- Move feet as quickly as possible while maintaining proper form
- Use arms for balance

SQUARE JUMPS

Develops: Power and agility for defense and dynamic 1-on-1 moves.

Equipment: Skipping rope, chalk or lines on the gym floor

Explanation: Find two lines that cross each other to make a quadrant. With two feet, jump back and forth over one of the lines as quickly as possible for 60 seconds. Rest for 60 seconds and then jump side to side for 60 seconds. Rest for 60 seconds. Jump forwards and backward and then side to side for 60 seconds and then rest for 60 seconds. Finally make a box by jumping forward, sideways, backward and sideways for 60 seconds and then rest for 60 seconds. Repeat.

Modifications: Use different combinations. Try to go faster, adding in more repetitions and sets. Try jumping on only one foot. Have a partner call out the direction.

Key Points

- Maintain balance and athletic stance
- Head and eyes up
- Move feet as quickly as possible while maintaining proper form (quick touches)
- Use arms for balance

FOAM ROLLER EXERCISES

Explanation: Foam roller exercises are great to do at the end of a workout to massage your muscles, increase your range of motion and decrease muscle soreness. Foam roller exercises should be built into all cool-downs. For each foam roller exercise you will "roll" the roller over the muscle for 1 to 2 minutes.

1 Sitting on the floor with your legs straight out and your hands on the floor behind you, place the foam roller under your hamstrings and slowly roll back and forth, massaging the hamstring muscle (on the back of your legs). Continue the massage from below your knee to above your foot, to massage your calf muscle

2 Lying on your stomach with your legs straight out and your hands on the floor in front of you, place the foam roller under your quadriceps and slowly roll back and forth, massaging the quadriceps muscle (on the front of your upper legs)

3 Lying on the floor with your legs bent and your hands stretched above your head, place the foam roller lengthwise on your spine and feel the stretch through your back and shoulders

4 Sitting sideways on the floor with your legs straight out and your hands on the floor to balance you, place the foam roller under your hips and slowly roll back and forth to just above your knee. This will massage the IT band (on the outside of your leg)

Other exercises: You can use the foam roller to massage and stretch any muscle in your body. The exercises above are common in basketball, but experiment with other muscles on your body to help with your recovery.

13

GOAL SETTING

Being good at something requires sacrifice and determination. To succeed at something, you need to first create wishes. If you want something to happen, you need to believe in yourself and think about your wishes often. Dream about what you want. Put up notes in your bedroom. Hang posters of your favorite player. Then once you have a wish, organize it into goals.

> *"It is harder to stay on top than it is to make the climb. Continue to seek new goals."*
>
> **PAT SUMMIT**

YOUR WISH

To make your wish a reality, you must understand what you want in great detail. Ask yourself the following questions. Answer them in as much detail as possible.

WHAT DOES YOUR WISH LOOK LIKE?

WHAT DOES YOUR WISH FEEL LIKE?

WHAT DOES YOUR WISH SOUND LIKE?

WHAT DOES YOUR WISH SMELL LIKE?

WHAT CAN YOU PUT UP IN YOUR BEDROOM TO REMIND YOURSELF OF THIS DREAM?

GOALS

For your wish to come true, you can't just dream about it. The next step is breaking down that wish into long-term goals and short-term goals. The long-term goal may be to make a school basketball team. The short-term goals are all the small things that you need to do to make the school basketball team. That may include increasing your vertical jump by 1 inch, going to a basketball camp or making 80 percent of your free throws. Each long-term goal should be broken down into at least three short-term goals. Write your long-term and short-term goals in a notebook where you can easily keep track of them. The more detail you provide the better your chances that your wish will come true.

Long Term Goal: Make the school basketball team next year

Short Term Goal A: Increase vertical jump by 1 inch before tryouts

Short Term Goal B: Attend basketball camp this summer

Short Term Goal C: Make 80 percent of my free throws before tryouts

DO IT!

The next step is to get out there and do it! Goals don't get crossed out overnight; some take many years to accomplish. You may fail at first, but if you try again and again and again, you increase your chances of succeeding. Failure is part of the process. Great players learn how to overcome setbacks and quickly return to practice. Keep your goals somewhere you can see them, revisit them often and don't be afraid to let others know about them so they can support you on the journey. Good luck!

Share your goals with others. You can feel vulnerable sharing, but the more people who know about them, the more help and support you can receive.

Keep it up! Once you achieve your short-term goals, create more until you reach your long-term goal.

ACKNOWLEDGMENTS

This book is a team effort. We'd like to thank Steve, Darcy and Stacey at Firefly Books for leading us through the publishing process, as well as our photographer, Christian, who spent hours getting the perfect shot. We also need to thank the athletes featured in this book who ran drills and struck poses over and over again.

Thank you to our families and friends who gave us their time, encouragement and even a few titles. To our colleagues, coaches, co-coaches and mentors — Ken Shields, Mike McKay and many others — you have inspired us and supported us throughout our careers. We cannot thank you enough.

The support of our team has brought our vision to life. Without them, it wouldn't have been possible.

We hope you enjoyed *Play Better Basketball*.

Kathy & Dawn

"One person cannot make a team."

KAREEM ABDUL-JABBAR

PHOTO CREDITS

Instructional photos taken on location at CORE Lifestyle and Recreation Complex in Kitchener, On.

Featured Athletes
Efosa Agbonze
Jody Brown Jr.
Leia Brown
Tyshawn Brown
Charlotte Clifford
Tanja Damjanovic
Josiah Davis
Jamal Hashi
Dayja Henry
Sydney Abedi Kabongo
Ahmed Radi
Madison Sousa
Madeline Weber

All photos are copyright © Christian Bonin, except the following:

AP Images
Elise Amendola: 166
Rick Bowmer: 184
Lachlan Cunningham: Cover
Tony Dejak: 8
David Dennis: 10
Sean D. Elliot: 130
Alex Gallardo: 66
Jerry Holt: 150
Ben Margot: 52
David J. Phillip: 5
Torrey Purvey: 74
John Raoux: 36
Marcio Jose Sanchez: 100, 187
Gregory Shamus: 6
Matt Slocum: 190
Winslow Townson: 90
Courtney Williams: 188

Icon Sportswire
Hector Acevedo/Zuma Press: 108
Brian Rothmuller: 22